Aggression in Man

Aggression in Man

by CHARLES BURKE

LYLE STUART, INC. / SECAUCUS, NEW JERSEY

To Marsha and Pamela

ACKNOWLEDGMENTS

Permission to reprint material from *Chagga Childhood*, O.J. Raum, granted by International African Institute, London.

A work of this kind owes much to the scholarship and labors of others. Many thanks to them all.

C.B.

Table of Contents

Preface

In recent years a number of writers have popularized their notions about man's fate being sealed by his inherited aggressive instinct. The study of animal behavior furnishes vivid illustrations of instincts operative in lower species. The implications are that man has been blind to his own animal heritage, failing to recognize his true nature, naively optimistic, beguiled by a heady romanticism that falsifies biological realities.

These arguments dismiss as fanciful the less spectacular accumulation of evidence in the social sciences. In particular, they have overlooked the role culture plays in shaping man's behavior. The history of cultural anthropology since Edward Tylor's *Primitive Culture* in 1871 has been an attempt to piece out our understanding of "that complex whole which includes knowledge, belief, art, morals, law, custom, and any other capabilities and habits acquired by man as a member of society." Enough has been learned so that I am hazarding the hypotheses elaborated here with slightly more determination than anxiety. The determination is my response to recent history, personal and public; the anxiety stems from the democratic nature of science: anyone may make a fool of himself.

What really prompted this effort, apart from the pernicious influence of natural science applied out of context, was World War II. War is the curse of our culture. Better men than I, and many of them, died then and have died before and since. Swept up in the war as a lad of seventeen, I have never been able to understand how it all happened. And each time I returned to my home in Marlboro, Massachusetts, and saw the names printed in black letters on the white memorial outside City Hall, the names of all the boys who died in that war, the names of boys I grew up with, names which I knew, almost every one, a question kept forming in the back of my mind. I had tutored one boy slightly older than I in algebra so that he could pass a test and become an air force pilot. He was killed over Germany. After all these years of looking at the memorial, of reading up and down the columns of names, the question finally took the form of the boy's name that I had tried to help, "Why did Danny die?" What follows has been an attempt to answer that question.

My intent is also to illustrate the integration of the cross-cultural method with the holistic analysis of a single culture. Essentially Abram Kardiner's thesis on cultural patterning is examined within the confines of the John Whiting and Irvin Child sample of seventy-five cultures in *Child Training and Personality*. Such a presumptuous undertaking at once suggests that I have entered scholarly domains beyond my depth. For the liberties I have taken with the field work and interpretations of eminent authorities, I feel I should tender my apologies for errors that are my own.

I also wish to express my appreciation to the Westport Board of Education and the Westport Education Association whose sabbatical-leave policy gave me the time to pull together the materials I have used in my attempt to present an alternative to the biological fatalism so persuasively presented to our youth, who are already pessimistic over man's future.

As a teacher, I must also thank all those students whose active curiosity kept pushing my own. The fact that students' questions act as a continuous spur to learn and think makes teaching a challenging intellectual encounter whose outcome is never entirely certain.

Nor should I omit my own teachers who were able to surmount the harrying distractions of the clerical pettifoggery—which drains teachers of their time and energy—long enough and often enough to give me the free gift of their learning.

Mention must be made of the critical, yet gentle, demurrers of Irvin L. Child. Without his support and encouragement despite our differences, this book could not have been undertaken.

And I should be remiss if I did not acknowledge the many courtesies extended to me by the staff of the Sterling Library at Yale University and particularly those associated with the Human Relations Area Files.

And finally, for reasons that are obvious to all those lucky enough to know her, to my wife Helen, may her patience be rewarded.

1. Instinct and Man

Plagued by war, the nations of the world are unable to arrest the mounting toll of innocent victims torn from their homes and families to be spent like an inflated currency in the purchase of peace at any price. But peace eludes the politicians, and all the treaties, alliances, concords, and detentes have served only to delay the resumption of open and violent conflict.

These periodic upheavals prompted Albert Einstein to write to Sigmund Freud in the summer of 1932. Einstein had been asked by the League of Nations' International Institute of Intellectual Cooperation to invite any person to exchange views on any problem that Einstein chose. He chose to ask Freud to respond to the question, "Is there any way of delivering mankind from the menace of war?" He added, "It is common knowledge that, with the advance of modern science, this issue has come to mean a matter of life or death for civilization as we know it; nevertheless, for all the zeal displayed, every attempt at its solution has ended in a lamentable breakdown."

How swiftly Einstein singled out mankind's most urgent problem. And how devastatingly accurate his perception proved to be.

Freud's reply in the fall of that year is especially interesting, given his lifetime of analysis of human motives.[1]

[1] Jerome Manis and Samuel Clark, eds., *Man and Society*, p. 678.

You are amazed that it is so easy to infect men with the war-fever, and you surmise that man has in him an active instinct for hatred and destruction, amenable to such stimulation. I entirely agree with you. I believe in the existence of this instinct and have been recently at pains to study its manifestations. In this connexion may I set out a fragment of that knowledge of the instincts, which we psychoanalysts, after so many tentative essays and gropings in the dark, have compassed? We assume that human instincts are of two kinds: those that conserve and unify, which we call "erotic" (in the meaning that Plato gives to Eros in his Symposium), or else "sexual" (explicitly extending the popular connotation of "sex"); and, secondly, the instincts to destroy and kill, which we assimilate as the aggressive or destructive instincts.

. . . You are interested, I know, in the prevention of war, not in our theories, and I keep this fact in mind. Yet I would like to dwell a little longer on this destructive instinct which is seldom given the attention that its importance warrants. With the least of speculative efforts we are led to conclude that this instinct functions in every living being, striving to work its ruin and reduce life to its primal state of inert matter. Indeed it might well be called the "death-instinct"; whereas the erotic instincts vouch for the struggle to live on. The death instinct becomes an impulse to destruction when, with the aid of certain organs, it directs its action outwards, against external objects. The living being, that is to say, defends its own existence by destroying foreign bodies. But, in one of its activities, the death instinct is operative within the living being and we have sought to trace back a number of normal and patheological phenomena to this introversion of the destructive instinct. We have even committed the heresy of explaining the origin of human conscience by some such "turning inward" of the aggressive impulse. Obviously when this internal tendency operates on too large a scale, it is no trivial matter, rather a positively morbid state of things; whereas the diversion of the destructive impulse towards the external world must have beneficial effects. Here is then the biological justification for all those vile, pernicious propensities which we are now combating.

. . . The upshot of these observations, as bearing on the subject in hand, is that there is no likelihood of our being able to suppress humanity's aggressive tendencies. In some happy corners of the earth, they say, where nature brings forth abundantly whatever man desires, there flourish races whose lives go gently by, unknowing of aggression or constraint. This I can hardly credit; I would like further details about these happy folk. The Bolshevists, too, aspire to do away with human aggressiveness by ensuring the satisfaction of material needs and enforcing equality between man and man. To me this hope seems vain. Meanwhile they busily perfect their armaments, and their hatred of outsiders is not the least of the factors of cohesion amongst themselves. In any case, as you too have observed, complete suppression of man's aggressive tendencies is not in issue; what we may try is to divert it into a channel other than that of warfare.

Freud's reply assumes a universal aggressive instinct that dooms man to eternal conflict. Freud's pessimism may be only a harsh realism, a fact of life and inescapable. In his own life, he had been deeply discouraged by World War I. In 1938, he had to be persuaded to flee for his life after Nazi police invaded his home in Vienna, and the Gestapo briefly held his beloved daughter Anna. Certainly the history of the world since World War II continues to lend support to Freud's bleak outlook.

Yet he had heard that somewhere races flourished that were not aggressive. He wished to know more of such people as he could not accept this flagrant contradiction to his belief that an instinctive impulse to kill and destroy encompasses all mankind.

Many writers have noted that Freud mirrored his time when he invoked the concept of instinct. Instinct was the usual explanation of behavior in the decades just before and after the turn of the century. Therefore, it is hardly surprising that Freud who had been so daringly inventive otherwise was conventional in this. Still, even here, to subsume all the instincts that were thought to govern behavior under just two, a life instinct and a death instinct, was an amazing economy of ideas.[2]

Freud's instinctivist explanation of human aggression has been reinforced by the writings particularly of Lorenz,

[2] Sigmund Freud, *An Outline of Psychoanalysis*, p. 20.

Morris, Storr, and Ardrey, encouraging misconceptions already widespread and mischievous. In *On Aggression*, Konrad Lorenz, an Austrian ethologist, finds man lacking the capacity to inhibit intraspecific aggression.[3] To Lorenz, without ritualized patterns of behavior controlling conflict found in lower species, man threatens his own existence. Man has "in his hand the atom bomb, the product of his intelligence, in his heart the aggressive drive inherited from his anthropoid ancestors, which this same intelligence cannot control."

In *The Naked Ape*, English zoologist Desmond Morris considers man above all a predatory primate, a killer ape dominated by biological urges. In Morris' swift reprise of evolution, the essentially peaceful, vegetarian primates become vicious, carnivorous killers, admittedly unique primates but primates nevertheless. To Morris, the history of Western man, the mainstream of evolution, illustrates the rapacious nature of the beast. Again, those "dead-end" cultures outside the mainstream distracted anthropologists from more profitable studies of our own culture.[4] Yet again, generalizations about man based on nontypical cultures are dangerous and biologically unsound.[5] Morris believes the real peril to mankind is our blindness to our basic animal nature.

Anthony Storr, an English psychiatrist, extends the same thesis in *Human Aggression*. To Storr, man is an aggressive animal. Exceptions have been reported, but "Most of these peoples . . . seem to be living under the dominance of neighboring societies who are more aggressive than themselves and have simply adapted a form of submissive adaptation in the face of perpetual threat."[6] Storr agrees with Morris that the marginal nonaggressive culture is far from typical and of no great significance.

[3] Konrad Lorenz, *On Aggression*, p. 49.
[4] Desmond Morris, *The Naked Ape*, p. 10.
[5] Ibid., p. 11.
[6] Anthony Storr, *Human Aggression*, p. 40.

In both *African Genesis* and *The Territorial Imperative*, Robert Ardrey, an American playwright, creates the image of man the killer, "a child of Cain," constantly improving his weapons, ready to defend his home to the death. Too many American social scientists are naive environmentalists in Ardrey's view; on the other hand, many European biologists recognize the soundness of a hereditarian position. Instinct is the hidden hand that moves us all and shapes our destiny, as it was in the beginning—according to Ardrey.

Ardrey's nemesis is the romantic fallacy.[7] So beclouded is our thinking by Rousseau's noble savage that a clear idea of man's true nature forever eludes us. Storr joins Ardrey both in an assault upon the romantic fallacy and in the recognition of the animal origins of aggressive instincts that betray man's nobler impulses. With Rousseau, man is good and society corrupts him. With Hobbes and Freud, man is evil and society saves him. With Ardrey, man is evil and not even society can save him. The Ardrey of *African Genesis* must rank as one of the great pessimists of all time. Morris and Storr are closer to Ardrey than to Rousseau, so if you are currently depressed, having read all three, it is perfectly understandable. Lorenz must be assigned to Hobbes and Freud, although he is really more hopeful than either.[8]

At least the camp of Ardrey, Lorenz, Morris, and Storr have provoked professional scientists into a more public discussion of the issues. Ashley Montagu collected a series of caveats published in 1968 as *Man and Aggression*. Lionel Tiger and Robin Fox have responded with *The Imperial Animal* (1971), an ethnocentric throwback amplifying Morris' mainstream image but even more imaginative with its sustained comparison of human social forms and the social interaction within a baboon troop. The most detailed criticism of the Ardrey-Lorenz-Morris text and an antidote

---

[7] Robert Ardrey, *African Genesis*, pp. 151ff.
[8] Lorenz, *On Aggression*, pp. 275, 279.

for much of the mysticism confusing even readers who should know better is Alexander Alland's *The Human Imperative* (1972).

Most of us assume that instincts (a now-obsolete concept), are an explanation of human behavior. Belief in instinctual processes supports the aggressive behavior we deplore. To explain violence as "just human nature" leaves us helpless and perpetuates the violence. Belief in a fixed unalterable set of givens in man is a folk myth written deep into our history by centuries of observations and descriptions of typical Western men and women.

Only comparatively recently have cultural anthropologists described men and women outside of Western culture who do not display the specific behavioral traits that are so often considered instinctive and natural in man. Insight into human behavior and especially human aggression is vastly enriched by comparison of Western man with man from non-Western cultures. Freud, you will recall, had wished to know more of those "whose lives go gently by."

The key to aggression is not locked in a "death instinct" or any other instinct but in the patterning of aggressive behavior that each culture transmits to succeeding generations. However, before we examine the anthropologists' concept of culture, both aggressive cultures like our own and nonaggressive, let us first take a closer look at the concept of instinct, a concept that may explain everything about human behavior—or nothing!

The concept of instinct has a long and controversial history. W. H. Thorpe, an authority on animal behavior, suggests it was the first biological concept the human race originated to explain animal behavior.[9] While the truth here cannot be known, an American college professor, Emil Wilm, traced instinct back to the Greek philosopher Thales. From the Latin *instinctus*, meaning impulse of instigation,

9 W. H. Thorpe, *Learning and Instincts in Animals*, p. 14.

the concept passed through the centuries eventually becoming part of the scientific lexicon of biologists and psychologists of the nineteenth century where it was confidently applied to man and beast alike. Charles Darwin devoted a chapter to instincts in *The Origin of Species*, concluding that instinctive behavior is the outcome of natural selection in the evolutionary process.

An early proponent of instincts, William James, whose *Principles of Psychology* in 1890 was the most influential book in the field at that time, wrote that instinct is "the faculty of acting in such a way as to produce certain ends, without foresight of the ends, and without previous education of the performance." [10] For James every instinct was an impulse, a tendency to act. Common impulses were blushing, sneezing, coughing, and smiling. Believing that all instincts were reflexes, he made no distinction between the two. As a result, his list includes snuffling, snorting, sighing, sobbing, gagging, vomiting, hiccuping, starting, sucking, biting, sitting up, standing, creeping, walking, imitation, speech, fighting, fear, sympathy, shyness, sociability, play, curiosity, acquisitiveness, modesty, cleanliness, jealousy, love, the hunting instinct, and the parental instinct.

James thought that higher animals, having more impulses, had more instincts.[11] Man, beset by the most impulses, had, therefore, the most instincts.[12] Every instinct may be an impulse, but not every impulse is an instinct. James coined the phrase "stream of consciousness" to describe the succession of mental events we all experience. Awash in that stream, impulses abound. If your impulse-life is anything like mine, countless impulses prompt behavior: shall I wash the car; let the dog out; fill my lighter; wind my watch; mow the lawn; clean the gutters; repair the fence; go to the library; feed the gerbils; increase my insurance; reseed

10 William James, *Psychology*, p. 346.
11 Ibid., p. 358.
12 Ibid., p. 347.

the lawn; or continue writing? It is simply inconceivable that all impulses are instincts.

Unlike James, most behavioral scientists and biologists attribute most of man's behavior to learning and the lower the species on the evolutionary ladder, the greater the influence of instinct on its behavior. The more generalized the organism, the more flexible is its adaptation to its environment. Omnivorous man makes more choices in nature's supermarket than the lion roaming the veldt or the leaf-eating gorilla hunched by a bush. As man is the least specialized of animals, his behavior is the most adventitious.

William McDougall was another early and outstanding advocate of instinct as central for understanding human behavior. To quote McDougall:

> We may, then, define an instinct as an inherited or innate psycho-physical disposition which determines its possessor to perceive, and to pay attention to, objects of a certain class, to experience an emotional excitement of a particular quality upon perceiving such an object, and to act in regard to it in a particular manner, or, at least, to experience an impulse to such action.[13]

His definition includes the built-in quality of an instinct, the perception of a stimulus, a particular emotion for each instinct, and the stereotyped response, or, at least, an impulse to act. Twelve instincts and their associated emotions were presented in 1908:

Instincts	*Accompanying Emotions*
1. To desire food	1. Appetite or craving
2. To reject certain substances or things	2. Disgust or repugnance
3. To explore new places and things	3. Curiosity
4. To escape from danger	4. Fear
5. To fight when challenged	5. Anger, rage
6. To have sex desire	6. Lust or sex excitement

[13] William McDougall, *An Introduction to Social Psychology*, p. 25.

Instincts, cont.	*Accompanying Emotions*, cont.
7. To care for the young	7. Tender emotion, love
8. To seek company	8. Loneliness, nostalgia
9. To seek to dominate	9. Elation, positive self-feeling
10. To accept inferior status	10. Humility, negative self-feeling
11. To make things	11. Feeling of creativity
12. To collect things	12. Acquisitiveness, pride of possession

Ronald Fletcher summarizes instinct theory in *Instinct in Man*, published in 1957. Reviewing the work of earlier theorists like James, McDougall, C. Lloyd Morgan, Leonard Hobhouse, and James Drever, he incorporates Freud's psychoanalytic theory of instincts and the work of Lorenz and Niko Tinbergen in comparative ethology into a contemporary theory of instincts. While a specific definition cannot be quoted, an approximate statement is that instinct comprises structural, physiological, behavioral, and experiential features established by heredity.[14] A partial listing of Fletcher's instincts includes breathing, eating, drinking, maintaining a comfortable temperature, sleeping, working, fearing, excretion, playing, curiosity, hunting, sexual activity, parental activity, and homemaking.

Viewing such a mixed bag, most psychologists have made more distinctions among this embarrassment of riches. Most of these distinctions are now considered either reflexes or simply learned behavior. Perhaps the only one to survive into the present as a continuing source of research and controversy is curiosity. No one had mentioned the fear of heights in infants—the visual cliff. Both will probably be regarded as learned; certainly curiosity is exploratory behavior associated with trial and error learning, perpetuated by occasional reinforcement. Today most psychologists, at least in the

---

[14] Ronald Fletcher, *Instinct in Man*, pp. 304–08.

United States, consider instincts to be more than impulses, more than reflexes, and rather different from either.

Both James and McDougall thought that instincts could be modified by experience and that behavior is the outcome both of instinctive impulses and the life history of the organism. Isn't this exactly what most of us believe? And yet the specialists in human behavior have turned away from this formulation. Why? Partly because by the 1920s, one scholar found "more than 5000" instincts included in the writings of students of behavior.[15] A word that means everything means nothing! Also, it no longer seemed persuasive to read that people behave in a certain way because that was the way people behave: the explanation did not explain.

Instincts among bees, birds, and fish control stable, stereotyped behavior patterns. Humans are so variable that no clearly identifiable fixed reactions were really comparable. The ancient analogy gave way.

Instinct was redefined so that more insight could be gained into the interaction between the organism and its environment. In recent years instincts have been regarded as complex, species-specific, and unlearned. Instincts are complex patterns of behavior. Blinking, sucking, swallowing are all reflexes as is the infant's ability to cry and the astonishing strength of his grasp. The fanning out of the infant's toes when a line is drawn down the sole of his foot from toes to heel is the Babinski reflex. Another is the startle pattern to a loud sound: lying on his back, the infant raises his head and legs, making a clasping motion with his arms.

If you wish to designate these reflexes as instincts as William James did, then the infant has an instinctual repertoire at birth. But most of the behavior usually proffered as instinctive occurs later in life and is much more likely to have been influenced by learning which precludes calling it instinctive by current definitions of the term.

[15] L. L. Bernard, *Instinct*, p. 175.

Instincts are species-specific. Each taxonomic subset has its own characteristic patterns of behavior that are clearly recognizable as typical for the species. Each species of bird sings its song and builds its nest in its own distinctive way. Rats, isolated from birth, will nevertheless mate without prior opportunity to observe normal mating, and the female will build her nest, give birth, and nurse her young.

Instincts are, above all, unlearned; they are the product of heredity alone. When Leonard Carmichael placed frog's eggs in a drugged solution, they were paralyzed but maturational processes led to normal physiological development.[16] When the eggs reached the stage at which they would normally swim as tadpoles, he placed them in pure water. They swam as well as a control group selected from among the same eggs and maintained under identical conditions except for the anesthetic. With no opportunity to practice, these tadpoles clearly illustrate unlearned, instinctive behavior.

As a corollary to species-specificity, instincts are also universal to a species. Any normal member of a species will exhibit the same instinctual behavior at the appropriate developmental level. We may confidently assume that any group of frog's eggs treated identically will swim as readily.

It seemed fruitful to develop new concepts that made more precise distinctions among classes of acts so that sneezing, jealousy, and submission were not treated as one. Hunger, for instance, was not labeled an instinct but a physiological drive. Tissues require oxygen, so breathing became a tissue need. Sleep is now a tissue need rather than an instinct. The gain may seem slight, if any, but a further distinction between a physiological drive based on tissue needs and an acquired drive stressed the role of learning more than the amalgam of instinct and learning. Even more

---

[16] Leonard Carmichael, "The Development of Behavior in Vertebrates Experimentally Removed from the Influence of External Stimulation," *Psychological Review*, pp. 51–58.

important, the details of acquiring particular behavior patterns were being discovered.

For example, an acquired drive, the need to achieve, has dominated the research of David McClelland for over twenty years. First, he developed a scoring system to distinguish high from low need-achievement by modifying the Thematic Apperception Test to include pictures of males in a variety of settings with another person or alone. Stories describing what was imagined to be occurring in the pictures were scored for the number of statements that reflected competition to meet a standard of excellence.

McClelland and his colleagues identified the cluster of traits that typify the male with a high need to achieve. High-scoring males assume personal responsibility for solving problems. Given a choice, they avoid situations where chance may outweigh results achieved by their own abilities and efforts. They are willing to take risks, but they limit the risk to an assessment of what they feel capable of actually accomplishing. And they seek direct evidence of progress toward their goal: sales figures, production quotas, lower costs—any concrete data furnishing immediate feedback. Their response to an ambiguous stimulus, a picture of a man in thought, points out how task-oriented they are. The male with a high need to achieve will usually see a man thinking about a problem connected with his work and, more often than not, solving it.

How do high achievers get that way? McClelland found that the fathers of high-scoring boys bossed them less; expected their sons to do well; gave them warmth and encouragement; and enjoyed their respect. Marion Winterbottom reported that mothers of sons with a high need-achievement expected their sons to have met over 60 percent of a list of accomplishments by age seven. Only about 35 percent of the accomplishments were expected by mothers of low-scoring sons. At an earlier age a boy with a high need-achievement was expected to do well in competition, to try new things, to try hard things for himself without asking for help, and to do well in school on his own.

Whether boys differ in the amount of innate, instinctive need for achievement can never be known. It is known that the manner in which parents treat the child and what they expect from the child in large part determines whether or not he develops a high need for achievement. Research in this area has progressed entirely without recourse to the concept of instinct.

But it was not just that psychologists could conduct research without the concept of instinct. As instinct was redefined, it did not stand up. The most telling argument in logic against an instinctivist explanation of human behavior is based upon the corollary of universality. If one mother rejects her baby, the maternal instinct falls; if one person commits suicide, the instinct for self-preservation dies; if one person is celibate, the mating instinct is sterile; one donation to a charity destroys the acquisitive instinct for getting and keeping; one pacifist, the instinct for fighting; one hermit, gregariousness; one kibbutz, territoriality.

The determined instinctivist may deny normality to every exception rather than alter intense convictions, but there are millions of instances refuting the universality of instinctive explanations of human behavior. In life, if not in logic, the real refutation of instinct lies in the incredible variety of behavior found in the cultures of men, rather than in the uniformity an instinctive origin requires.

Even in lower species, the concept of instinct has been seriously challenged. Kuo experimented with rodent killing in kittens.[17] Twenty kittens were reared in isolation, each in its own cage. In another group of twenty-one, each lived alone with its mother and saw her kill a rodent every four days. A third group of eighteen kittens lived with a rodent in each cage. Each evening until the kitten was weaned, the

[17] L. W. Crafts et al., *Recent Experiments in Psychology*, pp. 14–24.

rodent was removed and the kitten's mother was placed in the cage for the night. When weaning was completed, these kittens were isolated except for the rodent in each cage.

The kittens living with their mothers were further divided into three groups according to whether they saw their mothers kill a large albino rat, a medium-sized wild rat, or a small dancing mouse. The kittens reared with a rodent were equally divided, each with either the albino rat, the wild rat, or the mouse in its cage.

The kittens were tested by placing each of the rats inside the kitten's cage for thirty minutes every four days. On each testing the kitten was presented the albino rat, the wild rat, and then the dancing mouse. The tests continued from when the kittens were six to eight days old until it had either killed one rodent of each of the three species or had reached the age of four months. Each kitten, then, might have as many as ninety opportunities to kill a rodent.

Of the twenty kittens in the isolated group, only nine killed any rodent. If the albino rat was killed, the kitten also killed the wild rat and the mouse. Some kittens killed only the mouse without ever killing the larger rodents. In the group where twenty-one kittens saw their mother kill a rodent, eighteen killed a rodent, always killing first the species killed by the mother whether or not they killed the others. Among the eighteen kittens reared with rodents, only three killed a rodent, never the species they had lived with.

These are the facts; their interpretation will, no doubt, differ according to the bias of the interpreter. Since James and McDougall allow for the effects of experience, James, at least, might have argued that the middle group was habituated to rat killing and the others were not. This interpretation, however, would not explain the three kittens who saw rodents killed but never killed any themselves in 270 opportunities. The most generous interpretation favoring an instinctivist bias cannot deny that, if killing rats is instinctive, that instinct can be modified out of existence. If an instinct can be so totally inhibited as it was for twenty-nine out of fifty-nine kittens, can their behavior be better understood or better predicted based on the concept of instinct or on knowledge of early experiences? When nearly half the kittens do not kill rodents of any kind used in this experiment, the instinctivist explanation is, at best, highly unreliable.

A larger cat, Elsa, the lioness of *Born Free*, had to be taught to hunt. Reared by humans, as a mature beast she proved to be wholly inept as a huntress. Gradually after more than three months of training, she learned to kill. Her "instinct for self-preservation" would not have prevented her from starving to death.

Harry Harlow demonstrated how dependent upon normal mothering, mating is in rhesus monkeys.[18] At the Primate Laboratories of the University of Wisconsin, female rhesus monkeys were raised in individual cages where no interaction was possible. When it came time to mate them, the females spurned advances from males and were impregnated only with great difficulty. These females subsequently rejected their offspring. Maternal behavior for these so-called motherless mothers consisted of flinging her infant away or holding it underfoot when it sought attention. Whatever innate impulses of instinctual origins were totally eliminated: no maternal inheritance appeared. For the infants' safety, they were removed from their mothers. Were it not for opportunities to observe, touch, and learn from others, genetic gifts alone would lead to the swift extinction of the species.

Frequent comparisons of man and other primates, man's closest living evolutionary relatives, have linked man to the killer ape, suggesting that man's aggression derives from their instinctive ferocity. Of the four anthropoid apes—the gorillas and chimpanzees of Africa, the orangutans of Borneo and

---

[18] Harry Harlow and Margaret Harlow, "Social Deprivation in Monkeys," *Scientific American*, p. 144.

Sumatra, and the gibbons of Southeast Asia—the gorillas and the chimpanzees are closer in time to the origin of man than the orangutans and gibbons which the fossil record indicates evolved much earlier.

The greatest apes, the gorillas, are not killers at all, but vegetarians that spend most of their day munching on leaves, bark, and bamboo shoots. In the wild, mountain gorillas feed for two or three hours after awakening, nap for a few hours around noon, forage for a few hours as they amble toward a new nesting site, and turn in early.[19]

Their dentition reflects both diet and defense. The front teeth protrude from the fore of long **U**-shaped jaws, unlike man's parabolic dental arch with its sharper bite. The long canines, useful for tearing and shredding bark and leaves, prevent side to side chewing so large molars set in the massive jaws crush the leaves for digestion in straight up-and-down movements. Bony ridges on the skull anchor the powerful muscles required. Note that the horse's equally impressive set of teeth are for hay—and an occasional apple.

The gorilla's huge canines do not serve a carnivorous appetite but heighten his threat display. Consider the menacing spectacle of a gorilla frightening away a leopard. Imagine the hair-raising hoots of a silver-backed male beating his chest with cupped hands, throwing leaves and branches into the air, thrashing about as if eager to attack and finally crashing his hand to earth with a jarring thump. And all the while those dagger-like canines, bone white and glistening, signal a vicious potential. Even the smaller baboon, a lower species subsisting almost entirely on tender green grass shoots, can face down a predator and effectively discourage any attack by baring his canines without the gorilla's dramatic display.

As a result, the gorilla lives largely undisturbed—a placid, peaceful life of eating and sleeping. However, should a troop

[19] George Schaffer, *The Mountain Gorilla.*

of gorillas become alarmed, they usually flee to another part of the forest, not because they live under perpetual threat from more aggressive neighbors, but because they are naturally nonaggressive. If they chance upon another troop of gorillas who occupy the same range, there is no battle for territorial rights, only a brief encounter during which a female from one troop may join the other.

Both Morris and Storr assert that aggression in man is the expression of man's physiology, particularly of his endocrine glands and autonomic nervous system. The capacity for anger and rage are built into the structure of man's body, and structure implies function. James had said as much: Every organ has implicit within its design its proper function. The eye is made for seeing, the foot for walking. The argument appears irresistible. Adrenal glands are for raging. Yet consider the gorilla. With a similar physiology he rages not, except for occasional theatrical displays. The capacity exists in both, but its exercise is rare in the gorilla, relatively frequent in man. And far more frequent in some men than others. The question becomes, why does such a differential threshold for the expression of aggression exist among men with similar physiological structures? The answer lies partly in individual variations among men but primarily in the design of culture. Let me hasten to add that the same differences in the expression of aggression are also found among women and for the same reasons.

Finally, since so many claims for an aggressive instinct in man are based on aggression in animals, let us conclude with the views of two prominent biologists. No less an authority than Niko Tinbergen, whose studies of breeding in the stickleback (a fish) are classic in modern ethology, has stated that there is no general aggressive instinct in any animal species.[20] According to Tinbergen, members of different species rarely fight. Ninety-five percent of the fighting in

[20] Ronald Fletcher, *Instinct in Man*, p. 153.

nature occurs among males of the same species during the breeding season. And this fighting seldom includes actual physical combat but is largely one male threatening another who retreats, intimidated by his rival.

The other is J. P. Scott who summarizes the case for man: "There is no physiological evidence of any spontaneous stimulation for fighting arising within the body. This means that there is no need for fighting, either aggressive or defensive, apart from what happens in the external environment. We may conclude that a person who is fortunate enough to exist in an environment which is without stimulation to fight will not suffer physiological or nervous damage because he never fights. . . . We can also conclude that there is no such thing as a simple 'instinct for fighting' in the sense of an internal driving force which has to be satisfied." [21]

There is no denying that most men are aggressive. What is denied is that man's aggression is instinctive, arising necessarily from his genetic origins. If we are to account for man's aggression and both instinct and physiology are false explanations, then clearly human aggression is learned behavior, an acquired drive.

[21] J. P. Scott, *Aggression*, p. 62.

2. Culture and Man

If instinct can be set aside, if only briefly to consider alternatives, we can turn to the other major obstacle to understanding aggression—ethnocentrism. Ethnocentrism is the plural form of egocentrism; instead of the world turning around you, it turns around your group. Any group will do, as long as you are a member and believe.

A group of individuals is called a society; their behavior, all of it, is called culture. Many groups frequently affirm their superiority and identify themselves as "the people." Eskimo means "eater of raw meat"; their word for themselves, *Innuit*, means "the people." Navaho Indians call themselves *Dine*, meaning "the men." The Tiwi inhabit Melville and Bathurst Islands off the northern coast of Australia. Tiwi, their word for themselves, means, "we, the only people." For centuries, occasional visitors to the islands were driven off or massacred. Only the chosen people, the Tiwi, were permitted to occupy the island. Characteristically, ours is a government "of the people, for the people, and by the people"!

This widespread human inclination to regard one's own customs better than any others' has blinkered and hobbled our attempts to understand human nature. We have most often thought of world history as the record of our own origins. Earlier historians have written as if there were a direct, unbroken line from the first man chipping flint to our forebears sweeping in an arc around the Mediterranean, finally arriving in the New World shocked that some savages had somehow preceded us and incredulous that their civilizations rivaled our own. Despite current sophistication, we still prefer our art, our religion, our material culture, our language, our laws, our heroes, and our history to any other.

Does not that sweeping arc trace the rise of civilization, of history's mainstream, of the predominant people on the planet? Yes, and no. Western culture—including primarily Europe, North America, transplanted Europeans along the edges of South America and Australia, and scattered pockets in Africa, Asia, and Oceania—has created the most powerful and productive people the world has known. But a myopic vision of our own centrality has severely limited our opportunities to learn from other cultures and a fatal flaw endangers our future.

We have learned from other cultures, borrowing among other things foods, clothing, shelter, tools, and weapons. From the Indians of the Americas alone, we borrowed corn, the tomato, squash, the white potato, the sweet potato, pumpkin, turkey, avocado, pineapple, strawberries, tapioca, peanuts, cashews, lima beans, kidney beans, persimmon, chocolate, chile pepper, the vanilla bean, chicle, tobacco, moccasins, canoes, novocaine, quinine, ipecac, curare, new species of cotton, the hammock, and rubber.[1] Generally, we have adopted specific items. Seldom have we incorporated patterns of organization, social relationships, or values in any systematic way, although some of our young people are groping in that direction now.

Our flawed nature threatens our survival and all our works. Because we are an aggressive people, we have labeled mankind aggressive. And as our culture increasingly supplants others, we increase the risk of total destruction. As long as we continue to go our ethnocentric way, making the world over in our image, for so long will we fail to solve our fundamental

---

[1] Alvin M. Josephy, *The Indian Heritage of America*, p. 31.

problem: our penchant for violence that prompted Freud's pessimism. The paradox of Western culture is that the most productive culture the world has known is also potentially the most destructive.

There are cultures more violent than ours and less violent than ours. Obviously, we should learn from both. To do so, we must discard our ethnocentrism and adopt the objectivity and comprehensiveness of the anthropologist and the insight of the psychoanalyst. Despite our power and our number and despite its complexity, our culture is one among thousands. Without any question, all could benefit from selective borrowing. Each has much to learn from others. We have much to give and much to learn. We have developed the generosity to give; we have not developed the humility to receive. Our greatest gift is a longer life. In return, we may learn to enjoy it.

How to begin? From a world of possibilities where should one look and for what? Since we have the most to learn from nonaggressive and aggressive cultures, let us first look at the anthropologists' concept of culture and then at Freud's insights as they bear upon society and culture.

A culture is a society of individuals inhabiting a geographical area and living out their lives within a specific culture pattern. Culture patterns are relatively stable arrangements of material culture, i.e., all the things a people have, and nonmaterial culture, i.e., all the ways they behave and rules prescribing behavior. A culture is not a random assortment of possible elements but an amazingly articulated structure of meaningful relationships, only partially understood.

For example, your home is part of a tangled web of relationships, some quite remote and unanticipated. Every society has residence rules. A husband is sometimes required to live in his wife's community. In other cultures, the wife resides in her husband's community. Among the Dobu on an island off the coast of New Guinea, a married couple spend one year in the village of the husband's mother and other relatives and the following year reside in the village of the wife's mother. Still other cultures allow a free choice and couples may live apart from either parental community.

But residence is also dictated by economic considerations. Nomadic families range over a limited territory, moving as the animals move and as various fruits and berries ripen. In agricultural communities, the addition of new members adds their labor to the harvest.

In twentieth-century America, residence is so often dictated by company fiat that hordes of middle-level executives uproot their families and troop from suburb to suburb supporting a thriving real estate industry.

One consequence is that many youngsters today have a different sense of space. Where an earlier generation moved within a smaller circle of communities, a day's drive, today's adolescent will fly coast to coast to visit friends. Another consequence is that many youngsters have become disenchanted by the price in marital discord too many families have paid for a modicum of security.

Primitive cultures are by no means simple societies. In some ways they are more complex than our own. For example, among Australian aborigines the number of kinship terms far exceeds our meager list of relatives. Among the Arunta, one Australian culture, some idea of the complexity of their kinship system is indicated in the search for a mate. The proper Arunta marriage is defined as one in which the man marries his mother's mother's brother's daughter's daughter. Among the aborigines, the more relatives the better. When one is dying of thirst on the arid Australian heartland, it pays to run across a relative. This is one way of providing for sharing. Other nomads have a tradition of hospitality accomplishing the same end. The Bedouin on the Arabian Desert will share his food and tent with a stranger, and the Polar Eskimo will even share his wife. The Dahomeans of West Africa recognize thirteen different forms of marriage. In six forms, the children belong to the mother's clan; in the seven other forms the children will belong to the father's clan.

The customs of a people may be strange or repulsive, especially if the taboos of our own culture are violated. Cannibalism is abhorrent to us, but in some primitive cultures to eat an enemy is to gain his strength. Culture shock may discourage recognition of ingenious adaptations societies have invented to meet persistent problems. Many cultures have practiced female infanticide to effectively limit their population. The bestowal of infant girls achieved the same end more mercifully. Among the Tiwi, the man's prestige was measured in wives. All girls were married at birth, or even before birth, to promising young men in their late twenties. However, the girls would not reside with their husbands until fifteen years later. So most men became fathers when they were over forty at which time they could provide for their old age by incurring obligations from younger men upon whom they bestowed their daughters.

Primitive cultures are not primitive in language. They are preliterate: without a written language. Writing is rare and recent. In the whole history of man, writing may have been invented only three times: once in Egypt, once in China, and once in the New World among the Mayas of Yucatan and Guatemala. Before 4000 B.C., no writing existed anywhere. Since man has walked the earth for at least one million years, and possibly two, written symbols are of very recent origin. The vast majority of languages have been spoken, and linguists have never discovered an oral tradition less developed than any other among 2,800 known languages. All peoples possess speech adequate to express subtle nuances of meaning within the context of their culture. No humans anywhere are limited to a few grunts or gestures to communicate. Because of the complexity of their languages and the complexity of many other facets of their culture, anthropologists prefer preliterate to primitive when contrasting cultures.

Preliterate cultures also tend to remain relatively unchanged over long periods of time whereas literate cultures change more rapidly. Since Darwin, change implies adaptation, evolution. For too many theorists the evolution of advanced cultures from their primitive origins parallels the evolution of man from lower species. Cultures which have not changed, not advanced, are not evolving. Extinction is the common fate of sterile offshoots from the tree of life. In the evolution of life forms, more species are extinct than exist today. Adapt or die is the rule of life, and many preliterate societies have died.

This comparison of the evolution of culture and the evolution of living organisms is misleading. Only a remote analogy exists between ten thousand years of relatively rapid cultural change and 1 to 1.5 billion years of organic evolution. For man, during the long paleolithic period, the Old Stone Age, as he gradually refined his stone tools for thousands upon thousands of years amid the shifting glaciations of the Pleistocene, the really remarkable fact is that for 99 percent of his history, his culture hardly changed at all.

For well over one million years, prehistoric men lived by hunting and gathering—gathering first and hunting second since food was more easily picked than caught. Actually women did most of the gathering and provided most of the food. In the convenience of the supermarket, women are gatherers still. Men learned to hunt and fish together and fashion weapons to kill faster prey. For generation after generation, men radiated across the planet following the animals as the animals followed the changing vegetation. Men roamed in small bands, hunting a limited range and moving about with the seasonal ripening of edible tubers, fruits, nuts, and berries. The Bushmen of the Kalahari Desert in South Africa follow that way of life today. So do the Pygmies of the Ituri Forest in the African Congo.

The pre-eminent hunters, of necessity since there is nothing to gather, are the Eskimos. The Eskimos, being in the New World, represent a late specialization. Man arrived in the Americas about thirty thousand years ago. A group of Mongoloid hunters walked across a land bridge at the Bering Strait, probably trailing a herd of animals, and stepped into an uninhabited wilderness. Approximately eight thousand years later, men had hunted their way to the tip of South America. When the Eskimos arrived around two thousand years ago, the land to the south was already occupied, so they turned north to carve out a living from the ice, snow, and frozen tundra.

Long before hunters entered the New World late in the Paleolithic Age the races emerged, peopling the Old World with the varieties of man. Differences among men are essentially clusters of genes that have traveled together through generations of in-group marriages although reassorted in each generation. Four different processes alter the generations. Natural selection operates through the survival of the fittest. Your fitness, in an evolutionary sense, is the number of genes you contribute to the genetic pool, which is all the genes of all the members of your society. Your fitness, then, varies directly with the number of your offspring. Migration and intergroup marriage alter the generations as new genes enter the genetic pool influencing the physical characteristics of descendants. Mutations, those unpredictable genetic changes, are another source of generational change and are the familiar explanation of racial differences. The other possibility is genetic drift, the effect of random sampling, which possibly played a large role in band societies. Bands were small, limiting the number of possible combinations. The number of combinations was further reduced by fitness: some members produced more offspring. Certain genes, possessed by a few members of a band who did not reproduce, would be forever lost unless later contacts with others reintroduced identical genes into the genetic pool. Under these conditions, band societies may have produced relatively rapid evolutionary changes accounting, in part, for physical variations found today. One example is steatopygia, fat storage in the buttocks, found among women of the Bushmen and neighboring Hottentot.

Bands more isolated for long periods fostered the gradual emergence of physical differences through continuous in-group marriage of necessity. The Ainu, the caucasoid "Indians" of northern Japan, tall, hairy, and white, may be one instance. Bands in closer contact frequently encouraged friendliness by practicing out-group marriage, or if the groups were hostile, by raiding other bands and capturing women, children, and slaves. In either case, a genetic sharing increased the genetic pool and reduced differences among the populations.

Culture patterns show similar effects of isolation or contact. The more isolated the society, the more differentiated the culture pattern that emerged; the greater the contact with other cultures, the greater the sharing of elements between them. The structure of the Tiwi family is an example of behavioral differentiation in an isolated society. However, as with so many generalizations, there are exceptions. Far from simple transactions, exchange between cultures reflects the history and integrity of each.

Consider the Navaho and Hopi northeast of Flagstaff, Arizona, where the Navaho reservation surrounds the Hopi reservation. Approximately one hundred and thirty thousand Navaho, whose hogans (dwellings) can be seen south of Gallup, New Mexico, outside the reservation, far outnumber the almost six thousand Hopi. Both occupy lands in use prior to the arrival of the Spanish in 1540 under Coronado. The Navaho lived by hunting, gathering, and raiding the pueblos, the name the Spanish gave to the agricultural communities found in their search for the rumored gold of the seven cities of Cibola. The Hopi raised crops of corn, beans, squash, melons, and peaches and hunted small game, especially rabbits. The Navaho hogan is an octagonal log house topped with earth; the Hopi live on high mesas in stone houses piled on each other or so close they share a common wall. From the Spanish, the Navaho acquired horses and sheep and today most Navaho herd horses, sheep, goats, and some cattle while the Hopi still plants his crops, prays for rain, and sells his surplus to the Navaho for wool and meat.

After centuries of contact between the two cultures, borrowing has been slight. The Navaho practice some agriculture and the Hopi herd a few sheep. Also it has been suggested that Navaho ritual has been influenced by the elaborate ceremonialism of the Hopi. Navaho women are famous for their rugs, which they learned to weave from the Hopi. On the other hand, Navaho pottery is mud-colored and crude while Hopi pottery is among the finest in the world. The Navaho once made poor imitations of Hopi pottery but have since abandoned the effort.

The lack of sharing between the two tribes is based partly on hostility. Hopi pueblos were raided by "the people," and Hopi crops spread out at the base of the mile-high mesas were especially vulnerable. Also the prehistoric Navaho were much fewer in number limited by a hunting and gathering economy without the horse and gun.

The Navaho appeared from the north somewhere about 1000 A.D. Nearly paved with potsherds, the dusty streets of Oraibi, the oldest Hopi pueblo, have baked in the sun from that day to this. Evidence of their separate origins exists in the fact that no one has detected the slightest similarity between the Navaho and Hopi languages. Navaho and Apache languages have been traced to Indians of northwestern Canada. After fifty generations of contact between the Navaho and Hopi, each culture maintains its identity and integrity despite the enormous pressure Western culture exerts on both.

It is the changes that have occurred in the past ten thousand years, somewhere between .5 and 1 percent of hominid history, that suggest a parallel between cultural evolution and organic evolution. The past ten thousand years have brought rapid and accelerating change compared with man's prehistory. The invention of agriculture, probably by women who gathered seeds for food, enabled nomadic hunters to settle down. The development of food storage techniques increased the population which could inhabit an area, and the domestication of animals made hunting a recreation.

These changes were not sudden. Agriculture was marginal at first; hunting and gathering only gradually gave way to tending crops. The invention of irrigation added more to both the food supply and the population.

Food surpluses were the earliest form of wealth. In a hunting and gathering economy, the accidents of the chase and rainfall were followed by feast or famine. Living was literally from hand to mouth except for societies that had discovered lands rich in natural foods which could be picked like Polynesian breadfruit or harvested from the waters like the salmon which the Indians of the American Northwest skimmed from the brimming streams. Wherever food was abundant, populations multiplied, villages formed, and trade increased.

Larger villages brought about more varied social relationships than the smaller familistic bands. Occupational specialties, systems of authority, the formation of clans, status hierarchies, social classes—all became more extensive. As trade expanded, keeping count of obligations led to keeping accounts. And somehow, keeping accounts heralded the invention of writing. Why writing appeared so late and so seldom suggests that man is not as intelligent or inventive as he supposes himself to be. Only three hundred generations separate us from the origin of writing, which marks the boundary between prehistory and history. Those six thousand years have witnessed cultural changes on a scale and at a rate hitherto unknown.

More than any other, the invention of writing presaged the present. Writing preserves, accumulates, and shares experience. So does every culture, but writing adds a precision no memory can match. Other species have developed rudimentary tools, speech signs, and even teach their offspring; only man creates symbols. And only a few cultures, the written symbol.

Other cultures invented agriculture, irrigation, trade, villages, rules and rulers, but only our own developed a powerful technology derived from science. *Because* is the most important word in our language, because ours was the culture to exploit causation. Probably before writing was invented, some prehistoric Newton felt the fall of an apple and asked himself, "Why?" How many cultures discovered the "if . . . then" relationship? All perceived succession in the sun, moon, stars, tides, or seasons; but how many went beyond one event following another to one event causing another? The discovery that A causes B seems a short step from B follows A. If the seed is planted, then the plant follows. Was it not noted that the seed caused the plant to grow? And before the plant, the child? A new beginning for mankind was marked by the anonymous inventor who first glimpsed causal sequence.

Surplus food, writing, the idea of causality, a high need to achieve, an open class system to reward merit, villages where trade drew diverse peoples together—wherever this combination occurred, the conditions existed for borrowing, inventing, accumulating, and transforming culture. All societies borrowed, invented, and accumulated culture, and many were transformed under the impact of other cultures. From the American Southwest the horse reached the Plains Indians, increasing hunting efficiency and consequently their population. The gun arrived from the East, and where the horse and gun were first brought together, tribes with both drove their hostile neighbors away and hunted even more efficiently, spurring on an even more rapid population expansion. Our transformation has been generated internally through the emergence of a science-based engineering technology supporting a burgeoning population with ever-increasing demands for goods and services which we ethnocentrically label the rise of civilization.

Culture creates humanity. Not biologically but behaviorally, man's humanity, or lack thereof, is a product of his culture and his unique potentialities as a learner. Culture, mediated by parents, bends the twig and shapes the tree. Each culture recreates itself by fostering personalities which are responsive to the structure of rewards and punishments which characterize the culture. Obviously not in every child but in most, children learn to want for themselves whatever adults value whether it is to be a great hunter, a great warrior, or a millionaire.

In their play, children rehearse adult roles: a Bushman boy hunts insects with a miniature bow and arrow; a Hopi girl at Hano on First Mesa fashions a small cup to be fired with her mother's pottery; the American girl with her dolls pretends to be a mother, plays house, or in competition with others plays a real estate game like Monopoly. Boys find toy guns and cars irresistible.

Parents are the primary agents in socializing the child, teaching it through speech and example, affection and punishment from the moment of birth. In our culture Freud first pointed out that far more occurs in the transactions of parents and children than had previously been imagined. Particularly he noted that the amount of sucking allowed the infant, the severity of toilet training, and the resolution of Oedipal feedings had far-reaching and unanticipated consequences in the adult personality.

In the first year of life, the mother's warm nourishing presence as she suckles her infant provides him the earliest source of pleasure. Ever after, the mouth remains a source of pleasure whether through eating, kissing, drinking, chewing, smoking, or talking. Frustration of the infant's desire for oral gratification is the first denial, the first source of aggressive impulse which also finds expression through the mouth in biting and all forms of verbal aggression, especially that thinly disguised expression of hostility for the female, "son of a bitch," where the emphasis clearly falls on the last syllable.

During the second year, toilet training begins, and children learn that cleanliness is next to godliness. Mother demands a specified performance in a specified place at a specified time. Many children learn, and never forget, that there is a time and place for everything. If maternal expectations exceed infantile performance, an anguished mother readily creates an anguished child. High maternal expectations may lead to a high need to achieve, but at this time they can be a source of considerable frustration. The mother who badgers her child over lapses from grace adds increased resentment and hostility over physiological inadequacy or stubbornness to earlier aggressive impulses from oral frustration. It is not by chance that when anger is sufficiently aroused so many of us cry out, "Oh, shit!" or we say we are "uptight," a rather anal allusion.

By the time a boy approaches his fifth year, with toilet training behind him, his love for his mother knows no limit. According to Freud, the boy wishes to possess his mother exclusively, and as evidence of love returned, wishes his mother to bear him a child. Resentment of his father's successful competition for his mother's affection leads to fantasying the father's disappearance. Consciously the son still loves his father, but unconscious impulses urge death upon his rival. Fear that father suspects or even knows his secret and that a powerful father may punish him by cutting off his penis causes the boy to repress his Oedipal feelings altogether. The repression gives rise to feelings of guilt which form the basis of the child's superego or conscience. Whenever someone says, "You should be ashamed of yourself," unconscious depths echo in recognition of forbidden impulses. Consciously, the boy identifies with his father as a kind of "if you can't beat 'em, join 'em." In Freud's view, psychological masculinity results from the successful resolution of the Oedipus complex.

The Oedipus complex was central in Freud's thought and is easily the most offensive aspect of psychoanalytic theory.[2] That each father's son harbors a murderous impulse directed at his father was bad enough; but that at the same time he wished to replace his father in the marriage bed was unthinkable. Whether or not the Oedipal triangle exists as Freud described it, the universal taboo of incest suggests that frequent opportunity, potent impulses, or both must be resisted. In either case, Freud did establish that a reservoir of feeling and impulse exists beneath consciousness—the unconscious. In the unconscious, the life instinct and the death instinct, Eros and Thanatos, sexuality and aggression, have their origin. Freud thought these two great forces propel mankind. He named erotic energy libido. The destructive force remains unnamed. Beneath behavior lurks libido unrecognized.

It would seem to me that since sexuality is just one of the physiological drives, it could hardly be the sole source of motivation. Man does not live by sex alone. However, to Freud, because sexuality is so thoroughly regulated within our culture, our unconscious teems with frustrated sexual impulses. Another consequence of repressed sexuality is the subordination of other motives not allied with the driving energy of the unconscious. Freud also thought regulated sexuality was the necessary price paid for an orderly society. Through the mechanism of sublimation, repressed sexual impulses are redirected into creative achievements benefiting the society. Man generates more sexual impulses than are directly beneficial to society, so through repression and redirection, a creative force is harnessed to social ends.

Freud added another influence, sublimated sexuality, to the many others that encourage change. However, all so-

[2] Sigmund Freud, *An Outline of Psychoanalysis*, p. 97.

cieties regulate sexual behavior, yet all cultures do not relish novelty nor have they accumulated the immense variety of cultural elements we possess. Clearly, sublimated sexuality by itself is an insufficient explanation of cultural change. Still, given our cultural base achieved by invention and borrowing, sublimation probably plays some part in the overall process.

To Freud the other instinctive drive was destructive, undoing as opposed to doing, ending in death and the dissolution of the organism. On the contrary, not instinctive and not a physiological drive like sexuality, aggression is powered by emotion, by anger, rage, and fury. Emotions are motives, reactions to the process of socialization and patterned according to the sequence of experiences a particular culture imposes upon its children—the consequences of a particular style of child-rearing techniques transmitted through the generations as the "correct" way to raise a child. Acts by individuals which we call aggressive originate in hostile emotions aroused by parents in the course of training their young, unaware of the emotional consequences of that training. In general, the more harsh the training, the more hostile the child; the more indulgent the training, the less hostile the child.

The hostility is largely unconscious and felt on the level of impulse. Of course, anything may be said to exist in the unconscious, the perfect refuge for the undemonstrable. Yet the unconscious does exist, it was Freud's major finding however debatable its contents. Neglected since his death by the return to an emphasis on consciousness by many psychologists, it still works its mysterious way into behavior.

Not entirely a mystery, thanks to Freud, some unconscious processes are by now familiar. Three play important roles in sexuality: repression, identification, and sublimation. Each process represents more or less interaction between consciousness and the unconscious or, in Freud's words, between the ego and the id. In repression, the ego protects itself against anxiety by excluding threatening impulses from consciousness, not by deliberate suppression or intentional forgetting but by an abrupt transfer of distressing impulses from the ego to the id. Repression also blocks impulses from the id, keeping them out of the ego. In Freud's model of mental processes, repression functions in an intermediate zone between the ego and the id, where one shades into the other, which he called the preconscious. The ego itself gradually arose from the id paralleling the development of the individual. The ego or conscious self attempts to reconcile the often unreasonable and contradictory demands of external reality with the insatiable demands of the irrational id.

No wonder peace of mind is more sought after than found. In addition to the demands of reality and of the id, the harried ego is being constantly pressured by the superego as well, another contributor to the stream of consciousness. To illustrate, the struggle in the morning to get out of bed can be represented by the following internal dialogue:

> Ego, upon hearing the alarm: "Time to get up."
> Id: "Forget it! Go back to sleep."
> Superego: "Early to bed and early to rise makes . . ."
> Id: "Look you, I'm dreaming, and I don't want to be disturbed."
> Ego: "I'll just sleep another few minutes."
> Superego, ten minutes later in a voice reminiscent of one's parents: "It's getting late. You'd better get up."
> Ego: "All right, all right. I'm getting up right now."

The ego needs all the strength it can muster. The mechanism of identification enables the ego to draw strength from other people. Identification operates on both the conscious and unconscious levels. Consciously you may join a group and henceforth use the pronoun "we" to preface remarks such as, "*We* always support the Salvation Army." On an unconscious level, as indicated earlier, boys usually identify with their fathers and, similarly, girls with their mothers. Occasionally, as Erik Erikson, an eminent child psychoanalyst, observed, negative identification occurs, and youngsters strain to be as unlike their parents as possible.

In sublimation, libidinal energy eludes a censorious ego under the guise of socially approved activities. According to Freud, the intensity of interest the scientist, poet, composer, statesman, astronaut, or anyone else, for that matter, brings to his work is energy diverted from its original aim of erotic gratification to a socially productive purpose. Sublimation unified his explanation of our conscious preoccupations. Again that amazing and brilliant economy of ideas.

Three more mental processes—displacement, projection, and reaction formation—are significant for understanding aggression. Pity the innocent bystander, the universal victim of displaced aggression. About to lash out in anger, how often our blow strikes someone other than the one who enraged us. Attacking the instigator may bring painful repercussions, so our fury finds release upon some less threatening target, someone more vulnerable, smaller, less likely to fight back. Anyone will do. The employer humiliates his employee who soon has a furious argument with his coworker. The lieutenant chews out the sergeant who chews out the private who is spoiling for a fight. Who could be more innocent or vulnerable than the battered children brought to hospitals with broken limbs and extensive internal injuries and reported by their parents to have fallen from their cribs or down the stairs?

You will recall that Freud wrote there can also be a "turning inward" of aggression. The creation of the superego by the repression of Oedipal feelings is self-directed aggression, resulting in the formation of conscience, of feelings of guilt. Feelings of futility, of worthlessness, of hopelessness which persist accompanied by loss of weight and sleep are part of the psychiatric syndrome linked to psychotic depression. That depression is closely related to self-directed aggression is evident in the strong suicidal tendencies among the severely depressed. The symptoms of depression probably represent the disruption of normal ego states by impulses of self-directed aggression overpowering an ego made vulnerable by coping with unmanageable stress. Freud assigned to the superego, which has both a conscious and an unconscious component, the role of chastising the ego, fitfully whipping it into submission and depression. This is no doubt the source of his belief that all forms of releasing aggression are healthier than aggression displaced upon the self.

Even Anthony Storr, who, like Freud, believes aggression instinctive and dedicates *Human Aggression* to Lorenz, asserts that "the frequency of depressive reactions should make us reconsider our methods of child-rearing and our whole attitude to the aggressive drive within us."[3] Our methods of child rearing lay the base for aggression, but it is also significant that all child-rearing practices in all cultures are like pieces in a puzzle, shaped by all of the surrounding pieces reciprocally. Child-rearing practices are themselves the consequences of the overall design of the particular culture in which they occur: they are culturally patterned to replicate that culture. Adults, who have matured under the influence of a particular pattern of child-rearing practices, essentially fit the institutional roles that culture provides. It's an imperfect fit, of course, since the goals of institutions and the wishes of individuals are seldom congruent, producing more or less tension and conflict. Responses to tension and conflict reshape the culture, as a rule, very little, so that the puzzle that is culture is not a static but a dynamic design where each generation leaves its impress upon the accumulated cultural heritage.

Another of Freud's insights was projection. A form of denial, the individual often cannot accept emotional impulses so he attributes them to someone else. The preconscious and the id conspire to deceive the ego: the emotion is

---

[3] Anthony Storr, *Human Aggression*, p. 81.

projected elsewhere. A paranoid sees himself surrounded by assassins. In his distorted perception of others, he conceals from himself hateful impulses and legitimates his anxiety. The potential thief locks up everything in sight. The errant husband suspects his wife's fidelity. Another wife's tribulation over her husband's homosexual tendencies conceals her own latent lesbianism. Projection protects each from awareness of unbearable impulse.

In reaction formation, deception is compounded: concealment occurs by consciously adopting the exact opposite of one's threatening impulses. The ego fends off the internal threat by erecting sturdy bulwarks, testimonials of virtue, against the foreign devils. If homosexual impulses importune, one may parade a triumphant masculinity. If impulses to reject the baby beset its mother, maternal strivings may exceed every expectation. A painstaking honesty may conceal a liar's temptation; the too generous gift, a secret payment. In reaction formation, the best defense is a good offense.

The relevance of Freud's findings is that the unconscious is deeply involved in the patterning of aggressive behavior. Because the unconscious influences behavior in so many ways, some extremely subtle, Freud's insights are important variables in the socialization process as we shall see in the next chapter.

3. Psychodynamics and Culture

Each culture defines the proper way to raise a child. Social scientists call the process socialization. Whether the child will be picked up when he cries; whether dependence will be fostered; how early he is weaned; what he will be punished for, by whom, and how; whether he will be encouraged to walk, to explore his surroundings; what tales he will be told of good spirits and bad; whether he can "talk back" to his parents; what he must learn, must avoid, must do, and what he mustn't—every culture has norms which families more or less follow.

However, child raising is learned informally, and certain factors cause considerable variation among families in the same culture. For instance, the mores of social classes and ethnic subcultures will affect the manner in which children are treated. Within one family, a child will often be handled differently than his siblings because parents tend to learn as they go. And each child occupies a different position in the family constellation. The first born may enjoy a status no other can equal. He may be the living symbol of parental love or miscalculation. The last born may be privileged only to be displaced by each subsequent birth. Male children may be prized, or as among the Kikuyu in Kenya, girls may be especially welcomed since each will bring a bride-price paid in endless installments to comfort parents for their loss.

Children also vary in their response to parental demands, each being a slightly different sample of parental genes.

Despite individual differences arising from parental practices, birth order, social class, genetic variations, and a unique experiential history, there is still a series of experiences imposed upon most children that represents a particular cultural style and tends to limit the range of personalities found in each culture. And everywhere, "The child is the father of the man." The patterning of the child's emotions endures to motivate adult behavior and sustain a given culture's social institutions.

There have been two very different attempts to understand the effects of child rearing upon adult personality and institutional patterning. The first is associated primarily with psychoanalyst Abram Kardiner and anthropologists Ralph Linton and Cora DuBois. Working with a description of the Marquesan culture provided by Linton, Kardiner in *The Individual and His Society* traced a series of unsuspected relationships between child rearing, adult personality, and the patterning of Marquesan culture.

Before presenting Kardiner's analysis, a brief history of the Marquesas Islands may help to set the stage. One of the thorniest problems in teaching anthropology, as DuBois has noted, is to integrate the archaeological, historical, or diachronic dimension of culture stretching through time with the slice of life the ethnographer brings back based on firsthand observation, or at least secondhand accounts, of the living culture, the synchronic dimension. That integration will not be attempted here, but some knowledge of Marquesan history may at least lessen the strangeness of this unusual people.

The Marquesans occupy an archipelago just south of the equator in the central Pacific. All of the Pacific islands are grouped by anthropologists into three culture areas: Micronesia, Melanesia, and Polynesia. The Marquesans are one of the Polynesian peoples found in the great triangle that reaches from New Zealand in the southwest to Hawaii in the north and to Easter Island in the east. The Pacific islands were settled by Asiatic peoples with a relatively advanced culture who sailed east until this last of the uninhabited areas of the world was finally occupied by history's greatest sailors. At the time when the Mediterranean defined the limits of sailing skill in the Old World, these men challenged and conquered the immense Pacific.

On Nuku Hiva, the largest island in the northern group of the Marquesas Islands, Robert Suggs found charcoal from fires long extinguished and dated it by radiocarbon techniques at an astonishing 120 B.C.[1] Previous to his finding, it was thought that the Marquesas Islands were settled around 1000 A.D. In 1596, when the Spanish first discovered the Marquesas Islands, Marquesan culture had already had seventeen hundred years of development independent of any Western influence.

In 1596, in the usual way of discoverers, while looking for the Solomon Islands, Alvaro de Mendana sailed into a bay at Tahu Ata, an island in the southern group, commanding four Spanish ships. Outraged by pilfering of the natives who swarmed aboard his ships, Mendana ordered his crew to fire on them driving the curious natives ashore. Mendana followed, entered their village and taught the "Indians" a lesson.

Two hundred years passed before the next European visitor appeared, the great Captain James Cook in 1767. Again violence erupted, and more natives lost their lives. Estimates of the native population at that time by Cook and others who followed him were from 100,000 to 150,000. Only 150 years later, the remaining Marquesans were reduced to a scant fifteen hundred survivors.

The Marquesas Islands are volcanic in origin, and the tribes lived in green valleys separated by rocky escarpments

[1] Robert Suggs, *The Hidden Worlds of Polynesia*, p. 208.

that ridged the islands. War, cannibalism, and human sacrifice were all features of Marquesan culture. These were the classic savages of legend and literature, but nothing the Marquesans knew was as truly fatal as contact with Western culture.

At the close of the eighteenth and during the nineteenth century, ships from England, Spain, France, China, Russia, and the United States stopped at the Marquesas Islands. Nuku Hiva, closest to the whalers' hunting grounds, was a favorite stop. Whalers from New England refilled water kegs, stocked up on vegetables and fresh fruits, and occasionally pressed natives into service as crewmen.

Marquesan women were not the least of the island's attractions. Handsome and more than willing, Marquesan women took pride in their sexuality. A distinctive set of practices among the Marquesans was the erotic preparation of females for adolescent and adult sexuality consistent with the importance of sexuality in Marquesan culture.[2] In order to increase the sexual desirability of their daughters, Marquesan mothers used their lips to elongate the labia from earliest infancy. Enlarged labia were considered a mark of great beauty. In addition, from the time girls could crawl, vaginal astringents were applied daily up to the time of puberty. As many as nine native plants were used to extract herbal medications. Astringents were believed to shrink the vaginal canal, to strengthen the muscle tone of the vagina, and to reduce vaginal lubricity. At the same time, daily massages were employed to flatten the mons veneris to conform to Marquesan standards of physical attractiveness. Vaginal cosmetics were also applied to reduce the redness of the mucous membranes lining the vulva, to soften pubic hair, and to eliminate odors.

Deserters from the hardships of life aboard the whalers frequently cast their lot with the natives. The best known

---

[2] Robert Suggs, *Marquesan Sexual Behavior*, pp. 39–42.

was Herman Melville who jumped ship with a friend in 1840 and returned to describe his adventures in *Typee*, his first novel. The actual tribe on Nuku Hiva is spelled Taipi. He claimed to have spent four months as prisoner of the Taipi, who regarded him as a demigod because of his fair skin and reddish hair. Actually he was on the island less than a month—three weeks and five days to be exact.

In his novel, which recounts his entrance to the valley, Taipivai, his stay with the natives and his eventual escape, Melville included a vivid description of native women beautifying their hair with coconut oil. Could it be that Melville's account was the origin of our use of the same ingredient in shampoos sold today? Incredibly enough, Suggs found that Melville's experiences were part of Marquesan oral history on Nuku Hiva ten years ago and, no doubt, still are.[3]

Deserters armed with guns found their way to most of the inner valleys throughout the islands carrying diseases of all kinds. Venereal diseases spread unchecked, contributing to an already declining birthrate. Sailors who were put ashore in 1867 dying of smallpox are believed to have reduced the population of some valleys by as much as two-thirds. Wholesale deaths contributed to the disorganization of native culture. The birthrate plummeted.

By the end of the nineteenth century, little was left. Alcohol, which deserters had introduced, and opium and other narcotics from the Orient were available, furnishing escape from the culture which had crumbled around them. Drunken orgies, sometimes lasting for several weeks, were ended by the French who had assumed control of the islands and whose missionaries had tried to convert the pagans to Catholic Christianity.

At their peak before white contacts, the warring tribes inhabiting the valleys were separated by natural barriers, the

[3] Suggs, *Hidden Worlds*, p. 177.

mountainous ridges, that divided each island into separate, green, fertile pockets so that passage from one valley to another was possible only by sea or by one of the trails that crossed the uplands. Tribes in the same valley fought among themselves or fought as allies against tribes from a neighboring valley. In Taipi valley, only six miles long and half a mile wide, three tribes had been warring for generations. Between formal wars, individual headhunting, blood feuds, and small raids for human sacrifices kept everyone on edge against the continuous threat of attack.

Forts built high above the valleys were prominent in defense. Observation posts were manned against surprise attacks. War canoes were built for raiding enemy villages or for a desperate escape after a major defeat, which was very rare. Most combat was limited to the killing of a single warrior, each man trying to bring back the body of his victim whose name he would assume and whose skull would dangle from his belt.

Truces were frequent during festivals when war was taboo, and friends and enemies would feast together on guard lest a ceremonial priest suddenly suspend the truce to garner a few sacrificial offerings. Occasionally women and children were able to view a battle and cheer their tattooed warriors on. At other times women, children, older men, and the chief retired to a place of refuge to await the outcome of battle. No humiliation could equal the capture of one's chief.

Between raids, village life circled around the family of the chief, other leading families, and the feasts they provided. Eating had a special place in Marquesan culture. The Marquesans experienced occasional severe droughts sometimes lasting as long as seven years. Actual starvation occurred. During such a crisis, large double canoes would be built, and many families sailed in search of new lands. Almost all were never heard from again. Tribal priests were known to disguise their voices and to call out at night near dwellings that new lands had been found rich in hogs, breadfruit, coconut trees, and all one could desire. New canoes were built, and more families went in search of food and fresh water. This was probably how most of the Pacific islands were originally settled, more out of desperation in the eternal search for food than from curiosity about what lay over the horizon.

The Marquesans dug food pits twenty feet across and twenty feet deep in which breadfruit could be stored almost indefinitely to wait out a dry spell. They also limited their population by reducing the number of women in the society. They denied practicing female infanticide, and although Linton writes that it was probably kept from cultural notice, there is no reason to disbelieve them since they were quite open about every other conceivable horror. Females were frequent victims of forays by neighboring tribes. In intertribal warfare, any victim—man, woman, or child—might be seized. Slavery was not part of their culture so all captives were put to death, except for the very rare instance when an attractive captive was adopted. More females than males were captured and killed, resulting in a ratio of five males to two females in a tribe. Probably women and children were easier to overcome, but there is some reason to suspect that females were the victims of displaced aggression.

The imbalance of males and females in Marquesan society produced an unusual family structure, one in which a wife had more than one husband. Most plural marriages are polygamous: the male takes more than one wife. When the wives are sisters, accustomed to living together, the marriage form is sororal polygamy. Frequently wives are not sisters, and in some cultures a separate dwelling is provided for each wife. Among all the world's cultures, polygamy is generally more widely accepted than is our monogamous family structure. Still, even in cultures where polygamy is socially approved, few men can afford to support more than one woman and her offspring, so that in practice monogamous unions far outnumber any plural form.

A family in which the wife has more than a single husband is called polyandrous. Frequently the husbands are brothers, and the marriage form is known as adelphic or fraternal polyandry. Polygamy refers to both forms of plural marriage, polygyny and polyandry. Polygamy also includes the conjoint marriage form in which more than one husband lives in marriage with more than one wife. Conjoint marriage is the most unusual marriage form and existed only among Marquesans, Tibetans, Kandyans of Ceylon, and the Todas of India.[4]

Polyandry has often been confused with cicisbeism wherein a wife regularly grants sexual access to one or more men other than her husband, with or without his consent.[5] Cicisbeism refers not to a passing love affair but an enduring, stable relationship outside of formal marriage. True polyandry occurs when a wife marries more than one husband within a particular culture's definition of a proper marriage. True polyandry has unmistakably been practiced by the Bashi Lele of the Kasai in the Congo, the Kadara and Kagaro of northern Nigeria, the Paviotso Indians of North America, the Tu-la of Indochina, the Kandyans of Ceylon, Tibetans, and scattered groups in northern and southern India (the best known being the Todas), and, of course, the Marquesans.[6]

With the Marquesans, Linton suggests that *household* is a more accurate description of the basic social unit than is the term *family*. A Marquesan household typically consisted of a chief husband, secondary husbands, the wife, her children, adopted children, and old people. Only the most prestigious households enjoyed more than one wife, the

---

⁴ Prince Peter of Greece and Denmark, *A Study of Polyandry*, p. 508.
⁵ Ibid., p. 110.
⁶ Ibid., p. 507.

conjoint marriage form. In most households the husbands shared one wife. Only the poorest Marquesans were monogamous. Secondary husbands voluntarily attached themselves to a household.

Men did all the work. They built the houses and the ceremonial platforms in front of each house. They fished, gathered and cooked the food, made articles for use, and looked after the children. The more males in a household, the more wealth accumulated. A house with larger stones could be built for the firstborn, male or female, who at the moment of birth displaced the parents in authority. A larger stone platform could be constructed for ceremonials and greater feasts given to enhance the pride of the members in their household.

The wife had no work to do—other than to attract and hold the men together. All adult males in a household had sexual rights to the wife. A male also had sexual rights to his brothers' wives and to his wife's sisters if their chief husband consented. A skilled craftsman was likely to win his consent, because a wife's capacity to gratify her husband and to attract new manpower to the household played a significant part in the prestige of the household. As a result, there was a continuous competition for husbands among the women of a tribe. Female beauty was prized. Jealousy and resentment was keen among the women of a tribe. Many women had a special spirit, a *fanaua*, who could put a curse upon another woman or cause her to die during pregnancy or childbirth. The rivalry for leading males led to an emphasis upon breast shape as the breasts were important in attracting males and in sex play. Women refused to nurse their offspring because nursing kept them out of the competition and distended the breasts. The rationalization was that if children were nursed, they would be hard to raise. The rearing of girls anticipated their future roles.

Kardiner, in his analysis of Marquesan culture, concluded that the absence of oral gratification and the maternal neglect in general produced an unconscious hostility toward females.[7] This might account for the tendency of secondary husbands to let girls wander off where neighboring tribes could capture them, and also for the willingness of tribesmen to kill females as readily as males or even more readily if battle losses are counted and the ratio of five males to two females was maintained.

Kardiner also employed the Freudian mechanism of projection. In his view, religion, legends, mythology, and folklore receive their content from the projection of emotions generated in early childhood experiences within the family. Evidence of the unconscious hostility toward women exists in Marquesan folklore. There were many tales of female witches and ogres who abused and terrified children, stole their food, were cannibals and seductresses of young men. These inventions expressed in projected fantasy the hostile impulses repressed in the interest of social harmony.

There is no reason to believe that reaction formation or any other mechanism could not function in the same way influencing Marquesan institutions. It has already been suggested that displaced aggression could account for the preponderance of female victims, which has functional significance within the patterning of Marquesan culture.

Cannibalism is just one of the differences that separates our culture from the Marquesans. In far-flung isolation, the Pacific islands were originally visited only by birds, fish, and lizards. Early settlers brought chickens, pigs, and dogs and planted tree crops like coconut, breadfruit, and banana; but when crops failed and food surpluses were exhausted, there was nothing left that was edible on these islands but people. Hunger cannibalism could occur anywhere, even in the foothills of the Sierra Nevadas among the snowed-in and starving members of the Donner Party; but few settings in the world were more vulnerable to a crisis in the food

---

[7] Abram Kardiner and Edward Preble, *They Studied Man*, p. 216.

economy than most of the Pacific islands. The animal life found elsewhere just did not exist on the islands.

In times of real famine, Marquesans ate people—preferably from another tribe but not always. Cannibalism became linked to human sacrifice and to war. The capture of enemy tribesmen, the major motive for war, was specifically for sacrificial offerings to feed the gods and honor the dead. Bodies were slung up, hooked through the jaws or lips, sometimes while still alive, as a feast for the gods. A dead chief alone required up to ten human sacrifices to lift his spirit. The launching of a canoe was over the body of a victim in the belief that the canoe was thereby strengthened. Cannibal feasts occurred, and Linton believed even the women and children participated.

Kardiner points to cannibalism as a measure of food anxiety, not only the anxiety over a constant supply but an anxiety over being eaten oneself.[8] Fear of being eaten is transformed through reaction formation into a wish to eat others and institutionalized through war, sacrifice, and cannibalism. Tales of the cannibalism of the gods add to the recurrent theme of oral aggression.

All Marquesans were tattooed by an extremely painful process. An ironwood mallet was used to tap a bone comb into the skin and indigo rubbed into the bleeding wounds. Males were tattooed all over including the eyelids and tongue. Girls were tattooed from the waist down, on the arms and hands, and below the lips. Tattooing was done during adolescence. A great warrior would undergo the process again around the age of thirty. To endure such pain suggests that self-directed aggression has been institutionalized with specialists expert in the art. For eldest sons of wealthy households, a separate house was built for the occasion.

Despite an uncommon amount of sensuality among the

<hr>

[8] Abram Kardiner, *The Individual and His Society*, p. 224.

Marquesans, relations between the sexes were not characterized by tenderness and affection. Women were sexually aggressive and copulation was accompanied by biting and scratching. Men felt they were being exploited by women and on many occasions excluded women from their activities. Some jealousy erupted among the men when they were drunk. Occasional suicides among the men and women resulted from being rejected. Male homosexuality was common. And wives often sought more attention by pretending to be pregnant.

In Marquesan culture, Kardiner discerned a pattern.[9] Survival of the society required adaptation to severe drought by limiting the population. The particular solution, reducing the number of childbearers, established the conditions for a polyandrous family. The polyandrous family in the Marquesas Islands was a household in which sex was bartered for labor to add to the wealth and prestige of the household. As a result women were so busy being wives, their roles as mothers markedly diminished, and children received minimal attention and affection. Consequently, all Marquesans grew up with a distrust and hostility toward women that permeated their culture.

While Kardiner did not focus his analysis upon aggression, there is no lack of aggressive behavior among the Marquesans. Tribal warfare, human sacrifice, and cannibalism are only the most obvious examples of institutionalized aggression. Men from neighboring tribes also fought sham battles, taking turns throwing coconuts and stones. A well-aimed throw occasionally killed an opponent but most often simply knocked him down. Suicide and tattooing certainly qualify as forms of self-directed aggression, although the former is infrequent and the latter, universal. The female's *fanaua* existed to harm other women; men also injured or killed through cursing.

[9] Kardiner and Preble, *Studied Man*, p. 215.

Marquesan society was an open-class system. Any male could earn the status of a great warrior, a superior craftsman, or a priest. Even women could become priests, although not the high priest. A firstborn woman could become the head of her household or a chiefess ruling over her husbands, calling them to her, or dismissing them at her whim. A chief's position was not hereditary. A number of households vied for leadership by competitive feast giving to enhance the status of their households. Status striving is one way of sublimating aggression; another is work, and the Marquesans created a rich material culture, each item specially carved to indicate its owner's identity.

Where did Marquesan aggression come from? Essentially we have examined some of the ways it was expressed. How did it arise? The frustration of the infant's oral needs has already been mentioned. So has the absence of an attentive mother. No frustration over toilet training existed since little attention was paid to the child's mastery of sphincter controls. There was no basis in the family for the formation of an Oedipus complex where attachment to the mother was not allowed to develop and husbands care for the children. The development of sexuality was uninhibited in childhood, adolescence, and maturity. Impotence was unknown. Children were not burdened with unpleasant tasks; in the importance attached to a firstborn child, Linton considered the Marquesans quite child-centered.

If one frustration stands out clearly, it is the general maternal neglect of the child beginning with the refusal to nurse or, at least, a very brief nursing period denying the infant's need for oral gratification. Apparently a diffuse attachment to males develops and an ambivalent response to females. Females were more often used than loved. A deep-seated resentment at an indifferent mother fuels an aggressive drive that is channeled into the culture's institutional patterns. As Kardiner pointed out, through the socialization of the individual child, a personality is created that integrates many of the institutionalized practices within a culture.

Additional insight into Marquesan polyandry comes from His Royal Highness Prince Peter of Greece and Denmark who did extensive field work among polyandrous families in India, Ceylon, and among refugees from Tibet. He concludes *A Study of Polyandry* with his theory that the function of polyandry is to bind men together where a harsh natural environment requires continual mutual assistance for survival.[10] A disproportion of men and women is not enough: he cites the Moslem Moplas who have the same ratio of men to women as the Marquesans but whose Mohammedanism makes the polyandry practiced by neighboring Hindus abhorrent to them.

In most polyandrous cultures, women care for their own children so that polyandry is not necessarily linked to neglect of the maternal role. Another Marquesan custom, adoption, which was widely practiced, reinforced the mother's emotional distance from her child. E. S. Craighill Handy reported in *The Native Culture in the Marquesas* that children were promised long before birth, and no request was ever refused since refusal to allow a child to be adopted by another household was an insult. Adoption from wealthy households involved so great an exchange of goods that few could afford to adopt a son from the most prominent establishments. Through adoption, alliances between households and between tribes were formed. The firstborn son was always preferred, and his future labor added to the household, another incentive for adoption. The head of a household wanted many sons to assure the necessary offerings to elevate his status in the land of the spirits. Even after death, status striving is still a concern. Households whose sons had been adopted simply adopted other sons to replace them. Under these conditions, the mothers' attitude toward their

---

[10] Prince Peter, *Polyandry*, p. 568.

children seems understandably defensive. If polyandry functions to bring men together in strong bonds of unity, the institution of adoption as practiced by the Marquesans helped to alienate mothers from their children. A harvest of hostility created a culture both brutal and cruel.

Marquesan culture, from which Kardiner's theory originally stems, illustrates his theory that secondary institutions like folklore or religion are influenced by primary institutions that impinge upon the development of the child. Kardiner analyzed a culture's mythology to uncover hidden motives as Freud analyzed a dream to gain insight into the motivation of a neurotic patient. Kardiner attempts to understand a single culture through an intensive analysis of the life cycle of the individual in relation to the institutional matrix that shapes him and that he, in turn, shapes in response to his emotional needs.

Actually, Marquesan culture was not a particularly good choice. The culture that Handy and Linton studied in the field for nine months in 1920–21 was the dried, fibrous husk and broken shell of the coconut with the meat and milk missing. Little remained of the old ways. Information relied on recollection. It is difficult to discuss basic personality and theorize about Marquesan motives when no data on personality was collected. But Kardiner knew this and said so. The truth is that it was the best that could be done at the time.

In all, Kardiner applied his theory to ten cultures: Marquesan, Tanala, Comanche, Pomo, Alor, Navaho, Plainville, Tapirape, Sikh, and Ojibwa. In *The Psychological Frontiers of Society*, he published his analysis of Comanche, Alor, and Plainville culture. Plainville is the name given to a town of 275 people located in the central United States midway between east and west and between north and south. In other words, a very small sample of small-town America. Alor is the most thorough test of Kardiner's suppositions to date; since Alor the Kardiner approach has in his words, "ground to a halt," and is, at this writing, somewhat out of fashion.[11]

Cora DuBois went to Alor, a small island in the Indonesian chain occuped by Oceanic Negroids, and returned with a description of their culture published in 1944 as *The People of Alor*, including life histories of individuals with dreams and fantasies, and the results of personality and intelligence tests. Kardiner constructed a basic personality type deduced from the life histories, and Dr. Emil Oberholzer, a psychologist, described Alorese personality from Rorschach tests alone without knowledge of the biographies or the culture. Neither had seen the other's data, yet a surprising amount of agreement was found between the two accounts of Alorese personality.

The Alorese lack self-confidence and self-assertion. They are suspicious, sly, and mistrust everyone. Relations with others involve lies, deception, and disputes over financial obligations. Violent aggression is followed by complete collapse into ineffective passivity. There is a rather general acceptance of despair as a prevailing emotional tone as if here is where "Most men lead lives of quiet desperation." And yet severe depression is absent. The Alorese fail to plan, to look ahead, and any difficulty is enormously discouraging.

How did such a constellation of traits arise? In Atimelang, the village on Alor that was studied, men furnish the meat for the family which is a mixture of monogamy and polygamy. The meat consists of pigs, chickens, dogs, rats, and sometimes sheep and goats. In the Alorese division of labor, women furnish the vegetables and spend most of their time in the fields fighting weeds and tending their crops of corn, peas, rice, and squash.

Residence on Alor is patrilocal: a wife moves to her husband's village and into his house. Descent is patrilineal: sons inherit their father's wealth. Women do most of the

---

[11] Kardiner and Preble, *Studied Man*, p. 223.

hard work and are the center of many disputes over financial obligations. A wife is acquired through payment of a bride-price, which is common in Africa; but on Alor the dowry is also part of the marriage arrangements. These payments are made back and forth at regular intervals over many years, sometimes for the length of the marriage. The down payment before the marriage is part of the bride-price, exceeding any other marital exchange. Even after the marriage, it is common for a wife to refuse sexual relations with her husband over disputed financial arrangements. Marriages are unstable: half the men in Atimelang had been divorced.

And what of the children? The children of an Atimelang family were left at home while their mothers worked the fields. A child's needs were attended to by a resentful older sibling or a grandparent. Mothers do not appear to want children in the first place and do not appear to enjoy breast-feeding them. While the mother is tending her crops, anyone may feed the child. Thumb-sucking is encouraged to keep the child quiet. The mother may masturbate the child; brothers and sisters will quiet the crying child the same way. Frequently a child is shamed and ridiculed or sent on a fool's errand.

As the mother leaves for the fields each morning, the child may attempt to follow. Unable to catch up to his mother, he often throws a temper tantrum. The mother's reaction is unpredictable. She may comfort him, beat him, or ignore him. The mother's reaction is the child's dilemma: he never knows what to expect or what treatment he will receive. Maternal neglect and inconsistency contribute to the child's confusion and resentment.

In the folklore of Alor, common themes are childhood frustration and aggression directed at parents. Kardiner cites one tale in which a child is told to bring water in a bamboo tube to the mother from a distant spring. The mother punctured the tube so the child always arrives with it empty. The child keeps trying but he cannot succeed. Meanwhile the parents ignore him. In the same tale, at his matrimonial feast, the now-grown child presents his parents with food tubes filled with feces.

Interestingly, Alorese mythology includes spirits who are unpredictable. They may help anyone at any time and are always total strangers to those they have benefited.

Primarily Kardiner found the Alorese emotionally isolated from each other, filled with hatred, preoccupied with inhibiting aggressive impulses, consumed from within. Alorese aggression is all or nothing: fury is followed by paralysis of the executive function of the ego. Nothing happens. Much aggression is discharged in financial disputes and in marriage where quarreling is common. If a man decides to take a second wife, his first wife is furious and makes plain that if he can afford another wife it is because of her labor. After the argument, the first wife will frequently challenge the prospective bride to a fight and a free-for-all begins that may involve all the women of the village.

As with the Marquesans, the basic cause of Alorese aggression is maternal neglect. In this instance, the mother's role as food provider keeps her away from her children most of the day. The child shifts for himself, often feeds on scraps, is tormented by other children, and is ignored by adults. No one pays much attention to the child's development. He is not encouraged to walk or talk. Toilet training is a matter of indifference.

In Alor he is the norm. If he were in America, we would call him a rejected child. His bitter resentment, his troubles in school and with authority outside of school whenever he acted out his hostile impulses, we would attribute to parental rejection. But such a comparison implies more similarity between the two cultures than exists. It is difficult to see Alorese culture except in relation to our own. Ethnocentrism keeps creeping in.

The Alorese are very difficult to understand. Their

culture is so unlike ours. For one thing, they have been there a very long time. The island chain of which Alor is a part was like a highway for all of the peoples moving toward New Guinea, Australia, and much, much later to all of the Pacific islands. During the Ice Ages of the Pleistocene when ocean water was locked up in enormous, land-girdling glaciers, Alor was part of a land bridge connecting Asia with Australia and New Guinea. The earliest fossils that are considered truly human, that of Homo erectus who lived 500,000 years ago, were found on Java not far from Alor. At least two other early men were found on Java—Meganthropus and Solo man. Meganthropus was identified by a gigantic tooth; Solo man was a Neanderthal variety occurring much later. All three are extinct forms today, but their presence on Java indicates that the Indonesian island chain has been a home for man far back into the prehistoric period.

Alor's long time span and its gateway location has contributed to the elaboration of Alor culture. The people are Oceanic Negroid generally similar to the Papuan peoples of New Guinea and the natives of Melanesia. Chickens and pigs were brought from mainland Asia where they had been domesticated. Agriculture, especially knowledge of rice growing, has the same source. The corn crop is really unexpected since corn is a New World product. At the time Alor was visited in 1938, the islands were part of the Netherlands East Indies; perhaps the Dutch or earlier explorers introduced corn and other crops.

For Kardiner, Alor had to be a disappointment. The study of native personality reflected the complexity of Alor culture. DuBois and others who had followed Kardiner's pioneering efforts to synthesize his variety of psychoanalysis and anthropology fully expected that data on personality and on the culture pattern would reveal transparently simple relations between the two. The data on Alorese personality collected in eight, sketchy biographies and from Rorschach protocols did not clearly outline an Alorese basic personality. Individuals varied more than was anticipated. Was there, in fact, such a thing as a basic or modal personality?

The mode is a statistic used to indicate the central tendency of a distribution of data. It refers to the most frequently occurring score. The modal personality by analogy should occur most often in a population. The village of Atimelang on Alor that DuBois studied contained approximately 180 people. Were the four males and four females chosen really representative? They were selected because they were articulate and willing and because DuBois really thought they were representative of the average adult. But in statistics one does not choose from among the willing; the most accepted practice is to choose at random from all the members of the group being studied. A random selection should increase the chances that the most typical Atimelangers would appear in the sample.

As things stand, there is no way of knowing how representative of modal personality the DuBois sample was. If you think about it, it is rather sad that the validity of Kardiner's hypothesis hinged on data gathered from eight natives.

In the social sciences, when better data is not available, there is a disturbing tendency to use the data one has, on the supposition that any data is better than none. But is it? Bad data is worse than no data. When there is none, judgment awaits the gathering of valid data. Bad data, inaccurate facts, lead to errors in judgment. Kardiner's theory did not survive his analysis of Alor. What weakened Kardiner's position was his effort to make so much of so little, and his inability to persuade his colleagues that his psychiatric interpretations were not just flights of fancy, ungrounded in the data and unconvincing as proof. Harris summarizes many anthropologists' views: "In the Alorese case . . . we are left . . . with an ingenious but highly speculative psychoanalytic tour de force." [12]

Proof of relationship between child rearing and cultural design took precedence over Kardiner's holistic approach. A new method of attacking the problem of socialization and cultural patterning appeared: the cross-cultural survey.

[12] Marvin Harris, *The Rise of Anthropological Theory*, p. 440.

4. A Cross-Cultural Approach

There are basically two approaches to the study of child rearing and culture patterns. Abram Kardiner represents the first. The second is the cross-cultural survey. Instead of studying one culture in depth to understand how culture creates and complements individual character, two men, John Whiting and Irvin L. Child, tried to unravel the tangled threads of culture and personality in an entirely different way. Whiting, an anthropologist, and Child, a psychologist, planned and carried out a more systematic and, in fact, a simpler attack upon the problem. In a search for scientific generalizations that apply to all cultures, they examined not one or two but seventy-five cultures to assess interaction between socialization, adult personality, and cultural patterning.

In *Child Training and Personality*, they are more precise than Kardiner. Socialization is defined as behavior associated with five systems of child rearing: oral, anal, sexual, dependence, and aggression. Each system is analyzed twice and a rating from one to seven assigned by three judges working independently and unaware of the hypotheses being tested. The judges' ratings were added so that a minimum of three or a maximum of twenty-one could be assigned to any category. The judges examined only selected data on each culture; they were not familiar with the overall culture pattern of each. Ratings were assigned to represent the degree of initial satisfaction obtained by the child from each system. Ratings were also made for the degree of anxiety a child felt when parents attempted to alter the child's customary behavior. The first rating, called the initial satisfaction potential, may be thought of as a measure of parental indulgence. The second rating, called socialization anxiety, is a measure of parental severity when the time comes, as each culture defines it, to intervene.

Although three of the five systems chosen were influenced by psychoanalytic sources, the analysis relied more on general behavior theory and the testing of hypotheses by accepted statistical procedures. Psychoanalytic ideas were restated within the framework of learning theory in which reward and punishment considerably influence the frequency of behavioral events. Dependence and aggression were treated as independent systems. Each was considered an acquired drive that could be learned as dependent or aggressive behavior paid off in a given cultural context.

Judgments were also made estimating the age when serious socialization began. Age estimates exist for weaning, toilet training, modesty training, training in heterosexual play inhibition, and for independence training insofar as the data made such judgments possible.

The plan was to test for relationships between different aspects of socialization and customs surrounding illness. The customs related to illness represent Kardiner's secondary institutions: projections of emotional constellations generated in childhood. Since illness and death occur in all cultures and since the ethnographic literature is rich in details describing customary treatment and beliefs surrounding illness, Whiting and Child decided to use reactions to illness as a specific instance of the hypothesized relationship between childhood experience and adult behavior.

Accordingly, data was gathered on explanations and therapies for illness in the seventy-five cultures and sorted for the same five systems that were used to analyze socialization.

For example, judgments were made as to the presence or absence of oral explanations for illness, anal explanations, sexual explanations, dependence explanations, and aggressive explanations. The same judgments were also made concerning performance therapies (what treatments were involved) and avoidance therapies (beliefs about avoiding contact with dangerous substances).

With data on specific aspects of child rearing and upon illness, the search for measurable relationships could now begin. If a definite relationship could be established, one could begin to think about proof in an area where speculation reigned—gifted speculation to be sure but not proof as social scientists had come to define it. Kardiner's work suggested new dimensions of analysis and hitherto unimagined insights into cultural patterning, but beyond an informed imagination, proof—hard numerical data—did not exist in the study of culture and personality.

To appreciate the achievement of Whiting and Child, we need to understand the psychoanalytic concept of fixation. During a child's development, he may become fixated at any stage where excessive satisfactions or excessive frustrations heighten the significance of an experience. An experience which has become fixated lends an importance to that experience which it otherwise would lack. In Freudian theory, fixation may occur during the psychosexual development of the child: the child's progress through the oral, anal, and phallic stages. For example, frustration of a child's oral needs during the first year "fixates" the importance of oral activities that persist into maturity and theoretically into the grave.

Whiting and Child extended the concept of fixation to experiences other than oral, anal, and sexual—to dependence and aggression, in fact. But most important, they distinguished between positive and negative fixation, pointing out that excessive gratification and excessive frustration are two very different experiences for any individual. The chances are that very different consequences follow upon whether one has experienced all that pleasure or all that distress, a rather basic difference for a hungry infant, say, who is suckled or goes without. Positive fixation is the persistence of pleasurable reactions to events suggestive of childhood gratifications. Negative fixation is anxiety arising from events reminiscent of childhood distress.

Through the concept of negative fixation, Whiting and Child were able to establish a definite relationship between behavior associated with illness and anxiety which occurred during childhood socialization. The relationship was demonstrated twice: once for oral socialization anxiety and once for aggression socialization anxiety. In both instances high socialization anxiety is related to explanations of illness. Societies that are high in oral socialization anxiety usually have oral explanations of illness; societies low in oral socialization anxiety tend not to have oral explanations of illness.[1] Similarly, societies high in aggression socialization anxiety usually have aggressive explanations of illness; societies low in aggression socialization anxiety rarely have aggressive explanations of illness.[2]

The relationships are not perfect. They were not counting sticks and stones but complex societies. Precautions were taken to use only those societies where enough data was available for confident judgments. The relationship is real enough. The chances of error in accepting a relationship between oral socialization anxiety and oral explanations of illness are less than one in two thousand. For the relationship between aggression socialization anxiety and aggressive explanations of illness, the probability of error is less than one in two hundred.

A specific instance of the influence of child rearing upon one facet of cultural patterning has been demonstrated. Not

[1] John W. M. Whiting and Irvin L. Child, *Child Training and Personality: A Cross-Cultural Study*, p. 157.

[2] Ibid., p. 161.

once but twice. And proven, or as close to proof as social scientists allow. So cautious have they become that, in a technical sense, no single experiment proves but only tends to prove.

But beyond the demonstration of a definite relationship between childhood experience and cultural patterning, Whiting and Child's data on child rearing made possible other significant findings. Perhaps most important is the fact that the five systems evaluated are not interrelated for indulgence or severity of socialization. How parents toilet train a child has no relationship to whether they have indulged the infant's oral needs nor to parental reactions to childhood aggression. Each system varies independently of the others with the exception of the oral and dependent systems. The relationships here may stem from the fact that the judges used the same data to rate each system. Oral indulgence was seen as fostering dependence; low oral indulgence fostered independent behavior.

With this exception, there is no evidence that a culture is generally indulgent or generally severe in raising offspring. Instead it appears that in each culture there are specific responses to each system, sometimes indulgent and sometimes not. For example, the Tanala of Madagascar are at the mode for oral indulgence among the seventy-five cultures in the Whiting and Child sample. Yet for anal indulgence they score lower than any other culture. Tanala mothers carry their infants upon their backs but use no diapers. Infants soil their mothers' clothing which is difficult to replace. As a result, mothers begin toilet training as early as two or three months and severely punish the child who is not fully trained by the age of six months. This finding makes untenable the assumption that the amount of aggression in a culture has its origin in a generalized indulgence or a generalized severity. This thesis must be rejected as oversimple.

And yet I have no doubt that an aggressive drive is learned, that unconscious hostile impulses are generated in childhood, and that through displacement, projection, sublimation, and all of the defense mechanisms, aggressive impulses both shape and find release in a culture's institutions. Freud considered the unconscious to have no sense of time. In the unconscious, the past is continuously present. Impulses generated in infancy are undiminished in potency. Unlike natural energy which is created and discharged, impulses in the unconscious are never discharged but continue to channel the body's energy toward forgotten goals.

Where, then, is the source of aggression? Perhaps severe frustration in any single system will generate enough hostile impulses to last a lifetime. Will any system suffice, or is one system more important than any others? Are there identifiable effects of frustration for each of the systems? If we examine Whiting and Child's data on oral satisfaction potential, an interesting pattern emerges. For sixty-nine cultures where data was available, the three judges' ratings of oral satisfaction potential or initial indulgence add to eighteen for three cultures representing the most oral indulgence; to seventeen for three cultures; to a mode of sixteen for twenty cultures; to fifteen for eleven cultures; to fourteen for six cultures; to ten for three cultures; to nine for one culture; and to six for one culture.[3] And which cultures represent the least oral gratification? The next to the last with a rating of nine was Alor. The lowest rating was earned by the Marquesans!

Of sixty-nine cultures for which data was available so that judgments of oral indulgence could be made, the two cultures with the least oral indulgence were judged to be two that Kardiner had analyzed, the Alorese and the Marquesans. And aggression runs rampant in both cultures. Wars among the Alorese were put down by the Dutch. Now their aggression finds an outlet in continuous quarreling over financial transactions and in marital disputes leading to frequent divorce. The chronic warfare of the Marquesans was

3 Whiting and Child, *Child Training*, pp. 341–43.

eliminated by the French. Today the remaining Marquesans live in a state of almost total disorganization. They have forgotten most of their traditional culture. What was not lost through depopulation of the islands was forbidden by colonial administrators and clergy. Theirs is a marginal survival neither Marquesan nor modern. Having survived pacification, they sell copra and cater to tourists. With their culture shattered, alcohol and sex are major preoccupations. It could be argued that continuous escape and instant gratification are better than no goals at all, but it makes more anthropological sense to see alcohol as acquired from the West and sex as a highly developed feature of the original culture. Both survive as remnants of a meaningful past and as forms of protest and escape from an empty present.

But we are getting ahead of ourselves. A more systematic study of the Whiting and Child data on indulgence and severity of socialization may yield more clues to the origin of aggression in man and his cultures. If all five systems are averaged for indulgence and severity, the following cultures received the highest and the lowest ratings:

TABLE I
AVERAGE OF FIVE SYSTEMS OF CHILD REARING

LEAST INDULGENT		MOST SEVERE SOCIALIZATION	
Culture	*Average of Ratings*	*Culture*	*Average of Ratings*
Dobu	10	Dobu	16
Tanala	10	Ashanti	15
Ashanti	11	Chamorro	14
Chamorro	11	Chiricahua	14
Chiricahua	11	Kutenai	14
Dahomey	11	Rwala	14
Hopi	11		
Rwala	11		
Sanpoil	11		

MOST INDULGENT		LEAST SEVERE SOCIALIZATION	
Culture	*Average of Ratings*	*Culture*	*Average of Ratings*
Siriono	17	Tikopia	8
Comanche	16	Bena	9
Pukapukans	15	Comanche	9
Kwoma	15	Yagua	9
		Siriono	9

The averages are based on summed ratings for initial indulgence and severity of socialization for the oral, anal, sexual, dependence, and aggression systems. In other words, examined for overall indulgence or severity, the cultures in the table above were selected from the Whiting and Child sample of seventy-five cultures to represent the extremes of parental treatment. It can be seen that the same cultures were not judged most indulgent and least severe in socialization anxiety. Only the Siriono and Comanche are found in both categories. Neither are the same cultures found to be least indulgent and most severe, although there are more cultures in common for both of these categories: the Dobu, Ashanti, Chamorro, Chiricahua, and Rwala.

With data on seventy-five cultures and considering that the judges' ratings are approximations based on uneven ethnographic accounts of indulgence and frustration in the various cultures, it seems simpler to group the data by pairing those cultures which are most indulgent with those which are least severe in arousing anxiety and similarly by pairing cultures which are least indulgent and at the same time most severe in curbing behavior. Such a procedure, as demonstrated above, sifts out those cultures which received extreme ratings for each set of pairings.

Because of the traditional Freudian emphasis upon the first three of the five systems, it may be useful to present these. If only indulgence and severity of treatment are averaged for three systems—oral, anal, and sexual—the following cultures are selected:

TABLE II
AVERAGE OF THREE SYSTEMS OF CHILD REARING

MOST INDULGENT		LEAST SEVERE SOCIALIZATION	
Culture	*Average of Ratings*	*Culture*	*Average of Ratings*
Siriono	18	Siriono	7
Ainu	15	Tikopia	7
Baiga	15	Ainu	9
Comanche	15	Alor	9
Paiute	15	Chenchu	9
Pukapukans	15	Comanche	9
Trobriand	15	Lepcha	9
		Yakut	9

LEAST INDULGENT		MOST SEVERE SOCIALIZATION	
Culture	*Average of Ratings*	*Culture*	*Average of Ratings*
Tanala	9	Dobu	15
Dobu	10	Ashanti	15
Dahomey	10	Dahomey	14
Chamorro	10	Chagga	14
Western Apache	11	Chamorro	14
Rwala	11	Manus	14
Ontong Javanese	11	Tanala	14
Maori	11		
Sanpoil	11		
Chagga	11		
Ashanti	11		
Azande	11		

For three systems, the cultures which fall in both the most indulgent and least severe categories are the Siriono,

Comanche and Ainu. Children in the cultures receiving the least indulgent and the most severe treatment are the Tanala, Dobu, Dahomey, Chamorro, Chagga, and Ashanti.

However, since the averages may conceal extremes of treatment for a particular system which may be a source of considerable frustration for the children of a particular culture, let us examine the data on individual systems. As mentioned earlier, Whiting and Child found that cultures were not generally indulgent or generally severe.

Only the Kurtatchi and Yungar are in the position of being the most indulgent and receiving the least severe socialization in the oral systems. The cultures in which oral needs are most denied both in initial gratification and in subsequent severity are the Marquesans, Dobu, Alor, and Taos.

Only the Siriono, Bena, and Yagua appear in both the most indulgent and least severe categories for the anal system. The Tanala, Dahomey, Chagga, and Manus were placed on the least indulgent and most severe lists.

The cultures which were assigned ratings as the most indulged and at the same time received the least socialization anxiety for sexual behavior are the Siriono, Marquesan, and Pukapukans. The double disadvantage of minimal indulgence and severe socialization exists for the Wapisiana.

Since we are examining the Whiting and Child data for cultures which are singularly indulgent or harsh and our concern is especially for the origins of aggression, here are their findings for aggression.

The cultures paired by judges for being the most tolerant of aggressive behavior are the Manus, Dusun, Siriono, Comanche, and Murngin. Aggression was most frustrated among the Hopi, Paiute, Lepcha, and Chamorro.

What do the tables mean? Are the cultures which are most indulgent and least severe in regulating the behavior of their children the least aggressive cultures? Are the cultures

TABLE III
RATINGS FOR THE ORAL SYSTEM

MOST INDULGENT		LEAST SEVERE SOCIALIZATION	
Culture	*Ratings*	*Culture*	*Ratings*
Chenchu	18	Tikopia	6
Kurtatchi	18	Kurtatchi	6
Yungar	18	Ontong Javanese	6
Siriono	17	Flathead	7
Witoto	17	Malekula	7
Yukaghir	17	Papago	7
		Venda	7
		Warrau	7
		Wogeo	7
		Yungar	7

LEAST INDULGENT		MOST SEVERE SOCIALIZATION	
Culture	*Ratings*	*Culture*	*Ratings*
Marquesan	6	Marquesan	17
Alor	9	Dobu	16
Dobu	10	Baiga	15
Rwala	10	Kutenai	15
Taos	10	Taos	15
Chamorro	11	Thonga	15
Dahomey	11	Alor	14
Dusun	11	Chagga	14
Masai	11	Navaho	14

which are least indulgent and most severe in shaping behavior the most aggressive?

While Whiting and Child demonstrated that, in general, one cannot speak of cultures as always indulgent or always severe, there is one that comes close. The Siriono are in both categories of most indulgent and least severe for every table except Table III where they received a rating of ten for least

TABLE IV
RATINGS FOR THE ANAL SYSTEM

MOST INDULGENT		LEAST SEVERE SOCIALIZATION	
Culture	*Ratings*	*Culture*	*Ratings*
Ainu	16	Bena	6
Alor	16	Kwakiutl	6
Bena	16	Siriono	6
Siriono	16	Chenchu	8
Yagua	16	Kwoma	8
		Teton	8
		Tikopia	8
		Western Apache	8
		Yagua	8
		Yukaghir	8

LEAST INDULGENT		MOST SEVERE SOCIALIZATION	
Culture	*Ratings*	*Culture*	*Ratings*
Tanala	3	Tanala	18
Chagga	6	Ashanti	18
Sanpoil	7	Dahomey	17
Dahomey	8	Ontong Javanese	16
Manus	9	Chagga	15
Arapesh	9	Chamorro	15
		Dobu	15
		Lesu	15
		Manus	15

severe socialization anxiety and so were not included as representing an extreme in that category. And it happens that the Siriono are not warlike at all. The Comanche are not found as frequently on each table as the Siriono, but the Comanche may be considered second in overall indulgence and lack of severity in socialization, as indicated in Tables I and II. And the Comanche, as it happens, were classic Indian

TABLE V
RATINGS FOR THE SEXUAL SYSTEM

MOST INDULGENT		LEAST SEVERE SOCIALIZATION	
Culture	*Ratings*	*Culture*	*Ratings*
Siriono	20	Marquesan	4
Marquesan	19	Siriono	5
Pukapukans	18	Pukapukans	5
Trobriand	18	Comanche	6
Lesu	18	Ifugao	6
Baiga	18	Lepcha	6
		Marshallese	6
		Tikopia	6

LEAST INDULGENT		MOST SEVERE SOCIALIZATION	
Culture	*Ratings*	*Culture*	*Ratings*
Abipone	6	Kurtatchi	18
Tanala	7	Wapisiana	17
Wapisiana	7	Chiricahua	17
Ontong Javanese	8	Arapesh	16
Azande	8	Manus	16
		Rwala	16
		Western Apache	16
		Wogeo	16

warriors, renowned for raiding and trading captured horses.
Clearly, the Comanche contradict our expectations that they
would be a peaceful people.

Perhaps the explanation can be found in Table III where
the Comanche are not among the cultures most indulgent of
the infant's oral needs. Kardiner had singled out the frustration of oral needs among the Marquesans and the Alorese as
central to the development of their character. But the
Comanche received a modal rating of sixteen for oral

TABLE VI
RATINGS FOR THE AGGRESSION SYSTEM

MOST INDULGENT		LEAST SEVERE SOCIALIZATION	
Culture	*Ratings*	*Culture*	*Ratings*
Manus	17	Dusun	5
Siriono	17	Abipone	7
Comanche	16	Comanche	7
Dusun	16	Manus	7
Murngin	16	Murngin	7
Yungar	16	Marquesan	8
Balinese	15	Masai	8
Thonga	15	Siriono	8
Tiv	15	Trobriand	8

LEAST INDULGENT		MOST SEVERE SOCIALIZATION	
Culture	*Ratings*	*Culture*	*Ratings*
Hopi	5	Paiute	21
Ainu	6	Hopi	18
Paiute	6	Chamorro	18
Omaha	7	Jivaro	17
Lepcha	7	Kiwai	17
Chiricahua	7	Lepcha	17
Chamorro	8	Palaung	17
Nauru	8	Taos	17
Sanpoil	8		

indulgence, nowhere near the low ratings assigned the Marquesans and the Alorese. The Comanche also received a modal rating of fourteen for anal indulgence. Still, this hardly seems frustrating enough to account for the marked emphasis upon the warrior characteristic of Comanche culture.

Table VI indicates that the Comanche are indulgent of childhood aggression and do little to inhibit its expression.

But the same may be said of the Siriono who have no warriors. Clearly, a closer look at both of these cultures is warranted.

And what of cultures with the lowest ratings for oral indulgence other than the Marquesans and Alorese? The Dobu stand out as one of the five least indulged of the seventy-five in the Whiting and Child sample. And the Dobu are second only to the Marquesans in severity of socialization. The Dobu are also at the head of the list as the least indulged and most harshly treated for all of the cultures whether we examine all five systems of socialization or the Freudian triad (Tables I and II). Ruth Benedict described the Dobu in one of the most widely read books in anthropology, *Patterns of Culture*. A more suspicious, hostile, embittered people would be hard to find.

The Rwala, with the same rating for oral indulgence as the Dobu, are among the fiercest warriors of marauding Bedouin tribes of Arabia.

The Dahomey of West Africa were a military kingdom unmatched for slavery and warfare anywhere in Africa.

The Dusun are one of the tribes indigenous to North Borneo known for their headhunting. Note that the Dusun indulge aggression and are the least severe in socializing aggression of the seventy-five cultures.

The Maori of New Zealand and the Masai of East Africa are both infamous for their ferocity in war.

The gaunt Indians of Taos pueblo in New Mexico, wrapped in sheets like displaced Arabs, are also among those cultures low on oral indulgence and at the same time severe in socialization. Northernmost of the Rio Grande pueblos, Taos vies with Old Oraibi, Arizona, as the oldest continuously inhabited place in the United States. And like the Hopi, the Indians of Taos, who inhabit two massive pueblos which look like a sand-colored Habitat constructed long before the Montreal World's Fair, are an agricultural people. Tending crops furnished their living, not hunting and raiding. And like the Hopi, who are among the least indulgent in Table I for the average of five systems, the Indians of Taos also stand out in Table VI as one of the cultures which does the most to curb aggression in children.

I had the opportunity to witness how effectively Hopi adults control their children. Driving down a steep incline after a visit to Hano and Walpi on First Mesa in the summer of 1968, I stopped midway to talk with a cluster of youngsters. To my surprise they quickly surrounded the car; and with flashing eyes, they cased the car for anything within reach. Each carried a stone, and I soon pictured myself driving off in a hail of stones. As I asked them a few questions, I was wondering how I could extricate myself from this embarrassing situation: I could not drive off without risking injury to the Hopi children. Suddenly, I heard the noise of an engine behind me and turned just as a pickup truck rumbled down the rocky trail with two men standing in the back looking over the cab at the group of children. In an instant, the children dropped the stones, flattened themselves against the side of the mesa, and looked distinctly uncomfortable. The children's reaction to Hopi adults was even more surprising at the time than their aggressive curiosity.

The Chamorro of Guam are also among the cultures least indulgent and most severe for Whiting and Child's five systems. In Table II, considering only the oral, anal and sexual systems, the same is true. However, note in Table VI that aggressive behavior is not tolerated among the Chamorro.

It would appear that this data offers some support for Kardiner. The ten cultures which exhibit the least oral indulgence show strong aggressive tendencies, as in the Marquesans, Alor, Dobu, Rwala, Dahomey, Dusun, Maori, and Masai, or are among those cultures which are outstanding in the control of aggression, the Chamorro, and the Indians of Taos—and the Hopi.

No culture in this sample of seventy-five equals the Tanala of Madagascar for severe and early toilet training. In Kardiner's analysis of Tanala culture which Ralph Linton had investigated, Kardiner interpreted Tanala toilet training as training in obedience or, in Freudian terms, as training in repression.[4] In a strong patriarchal system where fathers had absolute power, sons were obliged to labor in their father's fields and by winning the father's approval received occasional gifts, a classical Freudian symbol for human excrement. Sons who rebelled against having to ingratiate themselves for paternal largesse were allowed to become warriors or medicine men. That is to say, if a son's aggressive impulses were unmanageable, he could become a warrior and periodically vent his aggressive impulses in a socially approved way. For "vent," read "displace" and Freud's relevance is clearer.

Medicine men were entrepreneurs who made charms to cure the sick. Associated with the charms were compulsive rituals that the ill must perform if they were to recover. Medicine men, without enough money to start a new lineage, went into business to direct the behavior of others: a form of positive identification. For his patients, whose illness represent a transgression, there was a distinctive Tanala style of repentance: to be obedient to the demands of the medicine man was to become well again.

Even more anal was the Tanala attitude toward wealth. Wealth was money, land, or cattle. With enough land, a son could begin a new lineage. Money was hoarded against the time when enough was saved to purchase land. Like money, cattle was hoarded. The Tanala used neither the skins, the meat, nor the milk. He didn't use dung for fetilizer nor were cattle used as draft animals. Cattle could be killed for sacrifices and funerals. Otherwise they simply represented a man's wealth, but unlike his money, his cattle could not be concealed. Every effort was made to conceal a man's money.

[4] Abram Kardiner, *The Individual and His Society.*

No one, not even the closest member of his family, knew where a man had hidden his money. Predictably, thefts of money and raiding for cattle were common.

No ostentatious displays of wealth occurred at any time. Food in the form of rice was always adequate. Most men worked the rice fields except for eldest sons and heads of lineages who supervised other family members. Although these men had more prestige, no one ate more than another. Conspicuous consumption did not foment jealousy and hatred.

On the other hand, rivalry for the father's favor divides brothers, who are in direct competition, except for the eldest son who enjoys a special status in this patrilineal society. Linton cites a typical legend which Kardiner interprets as the Tanala equivalent of the Oedipus complex. In the legend, brothers are in conflict. They steal the wives from one of them. He remarries and has a son. His son steals his father's wives back from his father's brothers. An uncle pursues the son. They fight, end up admiring each other's skill, and form a blood bond. Then they restore the wives to the son's father.

In the legend a man is treated badly by his brothers. In the end they are reconciled through the agency of his son who ingratiates himself with the father by returning his father's wives. The son makes no claim to his father's wives, which is not surprising in a society where the father's power is absolute. Kardiner views the Oedipus complex as a function of the institutional setting, not an inflexible law of nature.

After the oral indulgence that is average for the Whiting and Child sample, Tanala infants early experience an abrupt change. They learn to control themselves, and this becomes a lifelong pattern. Getting, keeping, and hiding wealth become lifetime goals. At the same time, aggression is controlled through a rigid social system where sons owe obedience to their fathers, and fathers give fair treatment in return.

Another culture in Table IV that warrants a closer look is Manus. The Manus are rated among the least indulgent and most severe in socialization anxiety for toilet training. When the Whiting and Child data are averaged for Freud's focal experiences, the Manus in Table II appear among the least indulgent and most severely socialized. In Table V they are among the most severely curbed for sexual behavior. At the same time in Table VI they are rated the most indulgent and are among the least severely socialized for aggression. For oral indulgence and oral socialization anxiety, they are average for the Whiting and Child sample. In sum, here is a culture on the other side of the planet which exhibits striking parallels to our own in their pattern of child rearing.

The Manus were studied by Margaret Mead in the 1920s, again in the 1950s to determine the effects of World War II, and again in the 1960s. She has made Peri village on Great Admiralty Island one of the best-known communities in the anthropological world. As British anthropologists have tended to study the peoples of Africa, American anthropologists have primarily studied the Indians of the Americas and the peoples of the Pacific. In the Pacific only the Beagleholes of the University of British Columbia come close to matching Mead's extensive fieldwork among preliterate cultures. And no one anywhere in the world commands her breadth of experience observing children growing up on Samoa, Manus, Bali, and among the Iatmul, Arapesh, Mundugumor, and Tchambuli of New Guinea. Trained in both psychology and anthropology, she brought to her fieldwork a woman's concern for the developing child not to mention an enviable gift for exposition.

This brief summary of Manus culture is in what anthropologists term the ethnographic present: life as it was lived when the anthropologist described the culture. Initially, the ethnographic present is 1938–39 when Mead gathered the materials for her book, *Growing Up in New Guinea*; later it becomes 1953 and 1964 when she resumed her study of the Manus.

The Manus live on the south shore of the large central

island in the Admiralty Islands north of New Guinea. A few Manus villages occupy the shores of smaller, adjacent islands. Trading is their primary activity. Occasionally they would war on competitors or go to war to support allies with whom they maintained profitable trading relationships. But the Manus were reluctant warriors. They saw war as a waste, disruptive of trade, and unprofitable. In the old days before war was outlawed, young unmarried men were enthusiastic. In a war, they could raid an enemy village, capture a woman, and bring her back to their village where she would be confined to the men's house. There she would be raped by every man in the village, and her captor charged fees for the occasion. An enterprising captor might take her on a tour of friendly villages to add to his income. The women of a village would kill her if given the opportunity; but the men made the most of this alternative in a society where wives were frigid and the spirits made all sexuality outside of marriage a sin except for the women of the enemy.

Monogamy is the prevalent marriage form. The Manus have a nuclear family numbering only the husband, wife, and their children somewhat like our own but with a greater sense of obligation to other relatives. Most common among the world's cultures is the extended or joint family which includes in the same household grandparents on one side or the other depending upon whether residence is patrilocal or matrilocal. If patrilocal, he will also have his brothers, their wives, and children; if matrilocal, he will also have his wife's sisters, their husbands, and children. While the Manus do not have an extended family, they are patrilocal: the wife moves to her husband's village where she is surrounded by his relatives and far from her own. Usually, a young couple begin their marriage living in a section of the house of a relative who has financed the marriage. Descent is patrilineal, further evidence of the importance of males. All the children of the marriage will belong to the father's clan.

A Manus must marry outside his clan. Members of the

same clan trace their ancestry back to a common male ancestor. Ideally, the father chooses a wife for his son from his mother's clan. Marriages are expensive: at her marriage the bride arrives covered in money in the form of shells and dog's teeth. Strings of shells dangle from her ears, her nose, her arms. Her breasts are wrapped in heavy bindings of dog's teeth. Her legs are covered with dog's teeth and over them are aprons heavy with shell money. The marriage will begin a continuous exchange of valuables involving all the relatives on each side. Relatives are obliged to aid one another: brothers and sisters are especially bound to assist each other in every way. Even a brother-in-law is a preferred trading partner.

The ghost of a recently deceased male, whose skull is kept in the house, enforces family obligations. The ghost brings illness or financial misfortune to family members who engage in sexual misconduct and obscenity or who fail to pay their debts, to help relatives, and to keep the house in good repair. Interestingly, it is a female medium who during the night communicates with the ghost and reports what he disapproves of and what must be done if the sick person is to recover.

The Manus are extraordinary fish peddlers. The Manus live by fishing and trading their fish for other foods, goods, and money to neighboring tribes. As a result, skill in trading is the measure of a Manus. Plying the coasts of islands nearby in a canoe, a sharp trader will return with pots, baskets, sago, yams, taro, betel nut, spears, fish nets, wooden bowls, and beds. And money: the worked shells and dog's teeth that is their medium of exchange. They even trade for the wood that goes into the making of their houses and outrigger canoes. Status among the Manus derives from fishing and dealing. Even the women do what trading they can, benefiting from traditional brother-sister exchanges. Wives of successful traders become more deeply involved and enter the network of debt relationships on their own.

The other avenue to status is by financing the marriages of younger men who are then bound to labor for their sponsors to repay the debt. Adoption is common so that more marriages may be financed. Most men are debt-ridden. Manus men fish to support their households, to aid their sisters, to escape debt, and to enter into profitable exchange relationships with others. The bigger the deal, the more status accrues to the dealer. The Manus seem like Colonel Sellers in Mark Twain's *The Gilded Age*, always looking forward to making millions. Among the Manus, one exchange representing a major transaction like a marriage may involve as many as ten thousand dog's teeth and hundreds of shells. Exchanges involving one hundred thousand dog's teeth are not unknown.

A financial leader in the village retains his status as long as he remains active in trading relationships. Only the continuous manipulation of wealth supports his prestige. Should he stop for reasons of age or illness, he becomes an object of scorn. If he boasts about the past, he may be laughed at. The only achievement that matters is the progress of current transactions. To sustain one's prestige, one must always be in a position to answer the question, "But what have you done lately?"

This driven people with their houses perched on stilts in a lagoon near their fishing grounds and no other resources nevertheless has the highest standard of living of all their neighboring tribes. All success is a personal success resulting from the energy and business acumen of the individual. Each man tries to meet the pace set by other men in his village. He struggles to maintain his position relative to the others. If he can improve his relative standing, his status increases and status striving is the Manus way. Wealth is what counts; no other avenue to status based on any other achievement matters. There are no priests, no artists, no craftsmen, only the singleminded pursuit of wealth.

Under these conditions men work hard. Most Manus are

worried, anxious, and irritable. Where failure is a sin, one mustn't lose track of one's creditors and debtors. No relationship is equal in importance to that of creditor-debtor. Typically, Manus men die early in middle age and seldom see their first grandchild.

Some men refuse to enter the race for status. They fish for themselves, trade for necessary items, and forego the route to success. Naturally they are considered strange to be satisfied with a bare subsistence when with a little effort they might make something of themselves.

And what of the children? A mother suckles her infant for a year and then weans it by tying hair to her nipples. Toilet training is severe. Parents view their child's excrement with horror and revulsion which is rapidly communicated to the child. So ashamed are Manus children that moving one's bowels is ever after a secret act that must be hidden. Boys learn they cannot eat in the presence of their brother-in-law or a future sister-in-law. Later, no embarrassment matches the shame of seeing or being seen by one's betrothed before the marriage. No bride may ever see her father-in-law unless a special feast given late in the father-in-law's life lifts the taboo. No husband ever sees his mother-in-law; even conversation between a daughter and her mother concerning the daughter's husband is taboo. In countless ways, children learn all the avoidances of Manus culture and the shame that was most severe during their toilet training is elaborated into a major form of social control regulating Manus conduct.

Sex also falls within the range of Manus taboos. Adultery must be publicly confessed or one risks sickness unto death or financial disaster. The spirits keep track of offenses; their vengeance is swift. Only a confessed sin is forgiven. Mead furnishes some insight into the male psychology when she cites as a male ideal the forcible rape of a victim, seized by the hair, and dragged into the bush. This familiar fantasy, only very rarely acted out, fuses sex and aggression and reveals not just the sexual frustration of the male but his considerable hostility toward the female. The female counterpart, which perfectly complements the male fantasy, was expressed by the Manus woman who said "That house is good in which there are two children, one to sleep with the husband on one side of the house, one to sleep with the wife on the other. Then husband and wife do not sleep together." [5]

The measure of a girl's shame over natural functions is revealed by Manus men. A girl's first menstruation is the occasion for a feast. Manus men believe that is the end of menstruation until her marriage. When it was explained that unmarried girls in other cultures menstruate monthly, the men replied, "Manus women are different." [6]

Freud's Oedipus complex has a strange career on Manus. Essentially the mother has her child to herself for the first year only. Then the father, home after fishing early in the morning, feels it is time he got to enjoy his child and also time that his wife got back to work. The father becomes the center of the child's life when the child is not out with his playmates. The child imitates the father and feels free to abuse the mother. Both boys and girls identify with their fathers during the period which Freud called the phallic stage based on his observations of our culture. If anything, the girl's development is complicated by her close attachment to her father which is disrupted when her mother makes her a grass skirt and introduces her to women's work while her brothers are out playing.

Manus children do not look forward to becoming adults. Becoming an adult is to bear great financial burdens while Manus childhood is one of uninterrupted play. Parents compete for the child's favor. Usually the father wins and becomes the child's favorite. Fathers teach their children to swim and fish and manage their own canoe which he builds for them.

[5] Margaret Mead, *Growing Up in New Guinea*, p. 168.
[6] Ibid., p. 158.

After the first year, wives have little time for their children. Wives are kept busy stringing beads for valuable ornaments to repay their brothers or for their husbands' use in exchange. Fathers are never too busy to entertain the children which he considers belonging to him more than to their mother. The child often sees the father's harsh treatment of his wife and naturally seeks the protection of his father who gratifies the child's every whim.

Where all property is worth money, property is highly valued. Children are taught early that they may not touch anything. Everything is owned by someone, and sorry is the child who touches the property of another. As a result, the mother may leave her beadwork on the floor in the perfect knowledge that it will not be disturbed when she returns.

Children are encouraged to be aggressive and self-reliant. The child sleeps when he wishes, eats on demand, and is free to go anywhere in the village, even to areas taboo to the mother. Children fight but are not considered as quarrelsome as their parents. The mother who contradicts her child or attempts to interrupt the child's play may receive a smart slap across her face.

Children play one parent off against the other. They do not lack for opportunities: Manus marriages are filled with hostility. The husband often wishes his wife would work harder. A man must marry, but the abrupt change from freedom to debt-slave rankles. Wives are convenient scapegoats. A wife resents the fish her husband gives to his sister. If a wife feels her husband spends too much time at his sister's house, she may accuse the sister of being his second wife, a grave insult. Since the married couple have never seen each other prior to the marriage, the marriage from the beginning is not based on mutual affection and appears to go downhill from the start partly because each member's primary obligations are to their own relatives.

Children are free to berate their elders. The aged do not have a privileged status. The children learn no respect for them or, in fact, for anyone. The children of leading men imitate the aggressive behavior of their fathers. If a creditor makes a demand upon a wealthy man, he will call in all his accounts and harangue his debtors. He will go round the village dunning his debtors and quarreling over the value of beadwork or grass skirts their wives made or find flaws in strings of dog's teeth. The children of successful businessmen indulge in similar emotional excesses and are often equally obnoxious.

However, once a young man marries, he learns humility. He owns nothing; he has had no part in paying for the betrothal feast. He is made ashamed not to have paid for his wife. He has no place to live, no skills with which to earn a living except fishing and building fishing boats. An uncle who has arranged the financing for the marriage by borrowing from all his relatives and drawing upon his own capital allows his nephew space in his house providing the new couple is quiet, and his nephew undertakes to repay his debt.

Unaccustomed to limitations as a child, he was essentially a free spirit. The beneficiary of unusually permissive parents, he becomes proud of his independence and, in fact, somewhat spoiled. Apart from a few avoidances learned very early, he frolicked from dawn to dusk until he was entirely at ease on land or sea and confident in his ability to fend for himself in competition with his fellows. As a boy nothing was required of him, nothing was expected, and nothing did he give. He had no chores, no role in financial dealings, no rituals to master, no legends to learn.

Suddenly, he is married, deep in debt, and demands are being made by relatives on both sides that he meet his obligations. The only way to retain his self-respect is to earn the money required. Any other course is shameful, so he fishes, trades and saves toward the day when he can proudly reassert his independence. The youth is caught between shame and pride, the two driving forces in a Manus male.

It is apparent, then, that among the Manus, childhood

aggression is sublimated into competitive achievement for financial gain and its attendant prestige. Whiting and Child in their data estimate the onset of toilet training at just over one year from birth. The parents' reaction to a child's feces is so stressful that shame is attached to both ends of the digestive system. Both eating and elimination unless performed correctly are a source of shame. Where property is sacred and wealth treasured, the anal system is the most likely source of Manus aggression which is then indulged for its functional significance in the adaptive style of the culture. Manus shame and Manus pride in a material prosperity both reflect their austere anal experience.

Early in her career, Margaret Mead discovered a remote Melanesian society with rather remarkable similarities to our own. The Manus were chosen quite by chance at the suggestion of an Australian district officer that they would be easy to work with. Also an interpreter was available from among the Manus workmen. Manus Island, as it is popularly known, was part of a mandated territory transferred from Germany to Australia after World War I. Manus adolescents before their marriage were often indentured for three years to work Australian plantations or to serve as houseboys or police boys at Rabaul on New Britain, the old capital of the territory before it was moved to Port Moresby on the Papuan Coast. The Manus made better police boys than houseboys. As houseboys, their dignity was frequently offended; being a police boy one could exercise some authority over others. During their work period, they learned pidgin English which they taught others on their return. Today English is the official language of Papua New Guinea.

If Western civilization is the mainstream of cultural evolution, history's chosen people, isn't it astonishing to find a neolithic culture in the far Pacific whose character and values so much resembles ours? If our culture, seen through ethnocentric eyes, is a singular and special creation, the preliterate Manus must seem an incredible accident. Proof that the similarity between the two cultures is not just distortion introduced by the observer was presented by Margaret Mead when she returned to Manus in 1953.

By an unpredictable accident of history, the two cultures, ours and theirs, had come into extensive contact during the Second World War. As a result, vast changes had occurred among the Manus which she reported in her second book on them, *New Lives for Old*. She describes the impact of over a million American servicemen who had passed through Manus Island, which had served as a supply depot during the war.

The openhanded American soldier did not treat the natives as "boys." Natives who worked for the Army were fed on the chow line with everyone else and had a sense of being treated as equals. American machinery fascinated the Manus who, it turned out, are gifted with a high mechanical intelligence. I don't think we can quite grasp the awe which the natives felt as airplanes, bulldozers, vehicles of all kinds, new foods, medicines, housing, equipment—all the material wealth of a modern army—suddenly appeared in their midst. And as startling as anything else was the attitude of the American soldier toward these incalculable riches.[7] To a native coveting a useful item, the American casually gave what was desired. Casually. As if their wealth was unlimited as surely as it appeared to be.

A Catholic mission had existed on Manus. The Manus had been told about the brotherhood of man, but they had never experienced it. To them it seemed that the Americans had achieved that brotherhood. Men could work together without quarreling, without being continuously disrupted by explosive rage. At times black American troops outnumbered white troops on the island. To be black was no disadvantage. The Manus saw that all men could live the American way. As

[7] Margaret Mead, *New Lives for Old*, p. 182.

they put it later, "All men are brothers, black, white, green, red men, all are brothers." [8]

When the war ended, many Pacific Island natives formed "cargo cults." A prophetic leader would arise and convince his fellows that if they destroyed all their property, ships and planes would return to the islands enriching the natives with their cargo as they did during the war. For many natives, these riches flowed from God, and their gods would not forsake them. When the cargo did not come, many a native leader was killed and the cult subsided.

Such a cult appeared at Peri on Manus. There it was called "The Noise." Ships were expected at any moment. They were rumored to have stopped already at islands nearby. The Manus pitched all their belongings into the sea and anticipated the return of the cargo. But, of course, nothing happened. Elsewhere natives had built replicas of airplanes and control towers thinking that when the great birds saw the little birds they would land on the clearings and their cargo would arrive. When the great birds did not land, the natives waited and waited.

On Peri and among the Manus in general, however, something quite different happened. A native leader, Paliau, conceived the plan to throw out much of the old culture and enter the twentieth century as a modern people. Paliau was a returned police boy from Rabaul. Combining his experiences with Europeans on New Britain with the experiences of all the Manus during the war, he envisoned all the tribes of the Admiralties as one people banishing intertribal hostilities. He also discarded the economic peonage where young men were bound to labor for their elders. Marriage by choice without the costly exchanges replaced the arranged marriage. Women were to be the equals of men. The old name-avoidances whereby one never spoke the names of one's in-laws or ate in their presence was abandoned. He instructed lay

---

[8] Ibid., p. 410.

preachers to teach a version of Christianity that differed from that of the Catholic mission on the island and to serve in their own church. Modern clothing and money replaced the old. A common fund was to be saved to finance community improvements. Local courts were to resolve disputes. Paliau's vision was not a piecemeal borrowing of selected elements from Western culture; he wanted complete modernization at once.

The young men especially were responsive to what became the Paliau movement. On some islands, the young withdrew and set up splinter villages of their own. In Peri, the young conspired to bring change without consulting the older generation. The war had really changed everyone's thinking. The older generation was ready to change and they resented not being consulted by the young. Before the generations were reconciled, all were swept up in the great expectations accompanying The Noise, a leader was chosen and the people of Peri left their lagoon, moved ashore and, in a great communal effort, built rows of identical homes in two groups on each side of a central square. At the head of the square, they built their own church where a lay preacher held church meetings twice a day to teach the "true" Christianity, according to Paliau.

Perhaps the greatest change was the desire to set up a democratic form of government. The people in Peri had no chief, no king, no council of elders before the war. Morality was maintained by the ghosts. Successful financial leaders established the model for a prestigious life-style hedged by taboos and kinship obligations. Now the taboos and the ghosts were gone. Everyone was to be equal, and democratic decisions were to be patterned on the old New England town meeting. Only the meeting was not just for passing budgets or making minor changes in a local tradition but for eliminating old customs and adopting new ones. Even the proper way to rear a child was a legitimate topic for a meeting. And with the emancipation of women came discussions of the desirable relations with kin and with men other than their husbands. For example, before the war adultery was infrequent, a sin punishable by the death of a relative from a ghost-brought illness. After the war Paliau said that adultery was tolerable if a wife were paid for her services. But the change was not working out: a husband's anger threatened his relationship with God—despite the payment. As one Manus put it, "We are trying hard to learn the ways of Western man, but one thing we have not learned yet, and that is how to commit adultery properly!" [9]

In New Peri, the Manus were conscious of living the "New Way." A school was set up and great hopes invested in the education of the children. Difficulties in the present were blamed on the period of transition. When the children grew up educated in the New Way, things would be different, it was believed. Frequent meetings were held in the central square after an evening church service. Participants addressed the community in Manus, Neo-Melanesian (pidgin English), or a mixture of both for about an hour, and then the community would disperse to their homes.

The Manus still live by fishing, but now one trades for money or works for wages by his own free choice. Gambling at cards is a common recreation for both men and women and a source of disputes. Since now all men are brothers, to be straight with God and man, a Manus must have no anger. Anger in the heart is the major sin, an affront to God who still brings illness and death. Quarreling is forbidden. Relatives are not to meddle in one another's arguments. With the experience of anger a clear sign of sin, a good Manus would deny himself even the awareness of his own anger. With recognition of one's own anger repressed, it is not surprising that Mead notes an increase in suicides and depression, both forms of aggression displaced upon the self.

In 1964 when Margaret Mead returned again to the

---

[9] Mead, *New Lives*, p. 318.

Manus, one measure of the extent to which they had increasingly accepted Western patterns was the school's Christmas program. The school put on a candlelight concert to which everyone was invited. The songs were tape-recorded for broadcast over the village radio to win support for the continued success of their school. Children in school write essays about astronauts and satellites. They know that Manus Island has a tracking station. And, without doubt, they now know that Americans have walked on the moon.

To account for the transformation of traditional Manus culture, Margaret Mead emphasized the part cultural discontinuity played in what she felt were revolutionary changes in Manus culture. In the past, the abrupt transition from the freedoms of childhood and adolescence were followed by the discontent of young adults who at marriage became debt slaves. All Manus, but especially the young men, were so impressed by the American example that wholesale change seemed both possible and desirable. Mead also stressed the advantages of a total change where each new institution is reinforced by complementary institutions whereby each reinforces the other.

Where one culture dominates another and imposes its values and way of life upon another, the expression "cultural imperialism" summarizes the consequences of culture contact under these conditions. On the other hand, if the people of one culture are so envious of the culture of another that they voluntarily cast aside their traditional culture in their haste to adopt the new, it seems to me that they have committed ethnicide.

The Manus fit neither of these concepts. American culture was not thrust upon them; neither did they transform their culture into a wholly new pattern. Certainly they made major changes and many of them, but there was a basic congruence between the two cultures to begin with. The attitudes of the men of both cultures had much in common despite entirely different historical origins. Only a fateful contingency brought them together. If an American GI were understood to say that a Manus could do a better job than he had been doing at some task, the Manus already believed that one could and should improve his performance. If an American said that a Manus should stand up for his rights, the Manus emphasis on independent individuality and quarrelsomeness corresponded. If an American suggested that to work and save and drive a hard bargain was the way to get ahead, the Manus understood.

This neolithic culture of Melanesian natives did not step into the twentieth century across thousands of years by building a little Levittown, donning Western clothing, and holding meetings in the democratic style. In many respects they were already there: many of our values, sentiments, and social practices had been independently invented by a small society on the other side of the planet without benefit of a large population, an industrial revolution, or control of vast resources in land. What is even more remarkable, if this is turned around, is that we of the West, the vaunted mainstreamers, differ so little!

And of special significance is the similarity not only in values but in patterns of child rearing. Both patterns are child centered with considerable indulgence of childhood aggression. Both impose strict controls upon toilet training and sexual behavior. Both are permissive. Both encourage independence and self-assertion. This is not to deny differences in emphasis nor a major difference like the role of a Manus father, but the similarities suggest there may be more than a chance correspondence between the similarities in patterns of child rearing and the similarities in cultural patterning.

At this point it is clear that the questions raised by the analysis of the Whiting and Child data have not been answered. In pursuit of the origins of aggression, we shall now turn to cultures marked by outstanding aggression. Representative of such cultures are the Dobu off the coast of

New Guinea, the Chagga of East Africa, and the Comanche Indians of the American Southwest. Our assumption is that the culturally patterned expressions of aggression exist to release violent impulses generated in childhood frustration. At the same time there is no denial that aggression has a functional significance for the historically developed pattern of cultural adaptation. Hostile parents do not raise hostile children for the fun of it.

5. Aggressive Cultures

East of New Guinea on the small volcanic island of Dobu,* Melanesian natives eke out a precarious living from the stubborn soil. On Dobu each cluster of villages linked by intermarriage is continuously at war with other villages and their allies by intermarriage. The Dobu are, in a sense, both endogamous and exogamous: one must marry within the villages of one's allies; at the same time one cannot marry someone within one's own village. Clans more important than the individual or individual families rule the village. Within the clan all members of the same generation address each other as "brother" or "sister."

In many ways, the nuclear family of the Dobu is subordinate to the demands of the clan. One clear instance of clan dominance is the ownership of seed yams. In each family the husband and wife own their own seed yams which each plants in their own garden. Both will work each other's garden, and the harvest will feed their family, but at the death of either, the seed yams revert to the clan. Where the natives are often hungry between harvests, the greatest dishonor is to eat one's seed yam, which is not only cause for

* All knowledgeable readers will be revolted at my presumption in rewriting Ruth Benedict's account of the Dobu. Consider that the decision to test Kardiner's hypothesis within the data furnished by Whiting and Child made an analysis of Dobu unavoidable; also that I followed her example and based the entire account on Reo Fortune's fieldwork as she did.

divorce but abandonment by one's clan. No one would lend seed yams to a proven fool.

The Dobu are a matrilineal society. Descent is traced through a mother's daughters. A clan on Dobu is known as a "susu," meaning mother's milk. The resident susus of the village are the owners of the village. After marriage the Dobu reside one year in the wife's village with members of her susu and the succeeding year in the village of the husband with his susu. Each couple lives in its own house with their children. In the father's village it is his house; in the mother's village it is hers. All of the houses surround a central graveyard where ancestral mothers and their descendants are buried.

Matrilineal societies are common. What is unusual about the Dobu is the pattern of alternate residence. In the village of one's in-laws, one is at a humiliating disadvantage. All of the in-laws are owners and address the husband or wife by their personal name which he or she may not reciprocate. Each must work their in-laws' gardens in addition to their own for the yams that are the basis of the Dobu diet.

Each is constantly on guard against the adultery practiced by his spouse among remote relatives in his own village. The black arts of sorcery and witchcraft are a continuous threat where suspicion of infidelity is often founded on fact. Adultery with a village brother or sister is a frequent cause for divorce. A wife in her own village, where she cannot marry, is a willing accomplice in adultery. Surrounded by her kin, she is protected from her husband's wrath. In a rage, he may pick up his belongings and return to his village, which constitutes a divorce. Divorce is five times more frequent among the Dobu than the Manus. His children will remain with their mother, and he will rarely see them again. He would not be reckless enough to risk illness or death from sorcery by returning.

As a youth, his marriage began when he overslept one morning in the house of his future mother-in-law. The Dobu boy is not allowed to sleep in his own house where his sister may be receiving lovers. He goes "night-crawling" in neighboring villages, moving from bed to bed as invitations are extended and accepted. Each morning he slips away before dawn and returns home. His intent to marry is signaled by being asleep when the girl's parents awaken. His future mother-in-law sits in the doorway blocking his escape. A crowd gathers. The young couple appear. The girl's kin stare at the couple, and the two are now considered engaged. The mother gives the young man a digging stick and sends him off to make a garden. From now on he is forbidden to use the personal names of the owners of the village. Nor can he eat or drink in their presence. Now he must prove himself by working hard in his new garden and the garden of his future parents-in-law. He also works hard for a year in his own village to finance the gift exchanges that inaugurate the marriage. The marriage occurs when exchanges of food and shells have been made between the susu of each village, and the two mothers-in-law, each in her own village, have placed food they have cooked into the mouths of their new in-laws, the girl's mother to the boy and the boy's mother to the girl. Henceforth annual feasting between the villages will validate the marriage.

Each susu expects the young to marry "out-husbands" and "out-wives" from different villages. In this way the matrilineal kin of a village protect their status as owners, and the unrelated marital partners are kept in their place. Each couple is entitled to privacy in their house and in their garden. Otherwise, the out-spouse is a stranger among enemies, never fully accepted.

Reo Fortune, whose *Sorcerers of Dobu* is a classic ethnographic account, felt that jealousy was the keynote of Dobu culture. So much so that suspicion, envy, and treachery dog their lives. If one man's garden yields a rich harvest of yams, he is suspected of having magically seduced the yams to leave other gardens for his. It would be more accurate to say that a Dobu knows he has done this. Where seduction is a sport and great status is given the man who has seduced many women, Dobu husbands and wives distrust each other even to the point where a man accompanies his wife to the bush while she defecates lest her departure be a ruse designed to assure her a momentary dalliance with a village brother. Or he carefully times her return. Each Dobu has potent love magic without which his or her efforts would be futile. Such secrets are bought and sold or inherited from one's mother's brother.

Each Dobu also has incantations to bring disease or death to one whose garden has been more productive than his. Spells protect fruit trees from theft. There are no accidents among the Dobu; each misfortune is the expression of someone's ill will. Poison is suspected in any food given by another. An unattended cooking pot is an invitation to disaster. One's garden must be constantly watched over and the yams protected by garden magic. The harvest is a carefully guarded secret lest another's envy be provoked.

Each man a sorcerer; each woman a witch: all capable of dealing death to others. Death for trespass, death for seductions, death for a bad debt, death for theft, death for insult, death for interference in an exchange. No wonder the Dobu are feared by the neighboring Trobriand Islanders with whom they trade. The threat of illness or death hangs over all the Dobu. The Dobu are never at ease in their own village; attack may come from any quarter. Even a sleeping wife may be just an empty skin as her spirit travels abroad working witchcraft on the unwary.

No wonder Ruth Benedict called them the dour Dobu. Smiling and laughter, dancing and feasting are rare in Dobu. Even when marriage feasts are given, each susu sits apart and exchanges hostile glances along with the required gifts of food.

When a man dies on Dobu, those suspected are the very ones closest to him. The first act of an intended killer is to befriend the victim, to work, eat, drink, sleep, and rest with him. For many months a close friendship ripens, then the killer strikes. Using the victim's personal leavings, nail parings, or something in personal contact with him, the false friend will cast his spell. If his magic is stronger than his victim's, the victim will fall ill to one of the diseases endemic on Dobu and become deformed or perish. A man with strong magic is known by his good health, his many seductions, his numerous pigs, and rich harvests. Losers, those with weak magic, have poor gardens, little success in trading, and less with women. A crippling deformity may well account for all of the above, but for the Dobu it is the clearest sign that one lacks a powerful magic.

If a man or woman becomes seriously ill, he or she is returned to the home village and susu. Should death follow and the deceased was the wife, the husband is excluded from his house, the ritual mourning, all property, even his children. He spends one year mourning his wife in her village. He blackens his body with charcoal, and he does not bathe for the full period. He works his in-law's gardens, eating unripe coconuts and the coarsest yams. Round his neck he wears a ropelike badge of mourning. At the end of the mourning period, he leaves the village never to return. His house is destroyed. His children remain in the village of his wife's susu. His son will inherit from his mother's brother; his daughter will inherit from her mother's sister. He will never see them again.

If a man dies, his wife spends her mourning period in his village. At the end of the year, she will depart for her village with her children. Her children may never reenter their father's village, nor will they inherit anything of his including his name which remains within his susu for his sister's children to inherit along with his gardens, trees, and above all, had he lived, his magic.

Among the Dobu, witchcraft and sorcery do not work at a distance so hostility is confined to a particular village. Except for young men moving from village to village in the early evening there is little traffic between villages where rumors of powerful sorcerers discourage visiting. A path around each village enables natives to pass by hurriedly without entering. Villages number only twenty-odd members, and the population was declining when Fortune studied the Dobu. Aggression, then, turns in upon each small village where essentially only one's relatives live and "those-resulting-from-marriage."

What fuels the fierce enmity the Dobu direct toward each other? Let us look to the children. What experiences earned the low ratings assigned to Dobu in *Child Training and Personality*? First of all, the child is unwanted. The child does not belong to the father but to his wife's susu. The child will learn his magic from his mother's brother and inherit his name and property when he dies. Another obstacle to parental affection is the fact that copulation between husband and wife ceases until the child is weaned. Despite Dobu prudery, they lead vigorous sexual lives and the child is viewed as a source of deprivation. Further, with each child the mother's beauty is said to decline, and she is no longer as sought after as she was prior to child bearing.

Birth occurs in the house of the mother's mother from which the father is excluded for one month. During that time the mother suckles the infant if her milk is sufficient. If not, the infant goes without since the Dobu make no provision for a wet nurse. At home, weaning is early. The mother rubs a nauseous substance on her nipples, and the infant is fed premasticated yams.

The Dobu practice "Spare the rod and spoil the child." Easily irritated parents are quick to vent their anger on their child. Toilet training is accomplished by shaming and slapping. The crying child is left to cry it out. Children learn early to expect little sympathy from their parents. Even as adults, shame is so attached to micturition that a Dobu in a canoe with others will go over the side into the water so as not to offend. All natural functions are secret and shameful.

The Dobu never invite visitors to share a meal. If a Dobu is given food, he turns his back on the givers and eats apart from them.

The anger that seethes below the surface in the Dobu is easily brought to a boil. Children imitate their parents. A child angry at his mother will do what his father has done: break his mother's cooking pots. Or if angry at his father, he will strike at his father's dog as he has seen his mother do. He learns that displacing aggression is safer than a direct attack, especially among the Dobu where retaliation in secret by magical means is a constant threat.

In Dobu where one suspects a friend since an enemy often befriends his victim, the children are born into a culture characterized by jealousy, suspicion, treachery, and ill feeling toward others. In the family, the child's earliest experiences prefigure his adult antagonisms. Unwanted, constantly thwarted and punished, he becomes an apt pupil when the time comes to learn letter-perfect the charms that will protect him and injure others. Among the Dobu, sorcery and witchcraft represent the secondary institutions that Kardiner predicted would be projections of the harsh socialization of the child within the primary institution of the family.

In Africa on the lower slopes of that continent's highest mountain, Mount Kilimanjaro, live the Chagga. For centuries Chagga chiefs waged war upon each other and upon the Masai who herd their cattle on the plains to the south, west, and north of the mountain. Farther north at the foot of Mount Kenya, Africa's second highest mountain, are the Kikuyu. *Ngai* or god rules over the Chagga, the Masai, and the Kikuyu. Each tribe also has another name for god. For the Chagga it is *Ruwa*, their word for sun as well. *En-gai* is the god of the monotheistic Masai. For the Kikuyu, *Mwene Nyaga* rests at the top of Mount Kenya after his daily tour of the world. The Masai fought the Kikuyu to the north and all but surrounded the Chagga. Our interest is particularly in the Chagga who, like most tribes in East Africa, herd cattle and are often lumped together by anthropologists as "cattle cultures."

The Chagga sustained hostilities among themselves and among the Masai by raiding for cattle. The Chagga also fought over water rights. An ingenious irrigation system carried water for many miles from mountain streams to their banana groves and gardens. Draining water from another's canals was cause for war.

With irrigated fields, crop rotation, and herds of cattle, sheep, and goats, the Chagga multiplied until every area of the mountain below the frost line was inhabited. Over the years tribesmen from the neighboring plains including the Masai joined the Chagga so that today they are genetically more varied in physical type than more isolated tribes. Contact with migrants from other tribes also enriched the variety of skills the Chagga possess.

Kilimanjaro itself was a landmark rising abruptly from the plains to an ice-capped height of over nineteen thousand feet. In all directions, tribesmen and caravans took their bearings from the mountain. Originally indentured laborers, now merchants and shopkeepers, men from China and India are found all over Africa and the Pacific. In East Africa, the Chinese and Indians were preceded by Arabs who have been trading up and down the coast for at least two thousand years and more, probably three thousand.

Long before the modern European annexed his lands, the Chagga prospered as a result of the abundant supplies of fresh water from the mountain. First the Germans ruled the mountain, and after World War I the British took over. Today Chaggaland is part of Tanzania. A council of elders replaced the chiefs in 1962. Interestingly, the son of a missionary, writing his Ph.D. thesis in anthropology in the late 1930s, saw clearly an aspect of Chagga identity that is still relevant not only for the Chagga but for those Americans who identify with Africans. O. J. Raum wrote: ". . . with regard to the color of skin, the original ideal of beauty was jet black. Black is still a sacred color and pure black animals are sacrificed to ancestors. It is true that at the present day many natives prefer light-colored girls in marriage, because white skin has become a sign of political and cultural superiority. But many protests are raised against this adaptation. One of the essential African qualities is the black skin. It becomes a symbol in the fight for cultural and political recognition." [1]

Originally the Chagga acquired their animals, most of their crops, ironworking, their political and military organization, and probably their irrigation from immigrants from the north in contact with the cultures of the Nile and the Near East. Their favorite crop is the banana. Twenty-one varieties are grown, eleven for brewing liquor or for cattle fodder. If twenty-one seems an unlikely number because it is far too large, the Ganda north of Lake Victoria cultivate over two hundred varieties of banana. Next in importance is Eleusine, a grain from which the Chagga brew their beer. Beer is drunk daily by all Chagga and has been said to be the real reason for the irrigation since the Eleusine requires so much water. Gifts of beer are part of the bride-price, and hundreds of gallons of beer are consumed at a wedding.

The Chagga are polygamous. A man receives his first wife's permission to take a second wife, his second wife's permission to take a third wife, and so on. Wives are from other clans. However among the Chagga, clans do not have the divisive importance that they do among the Dobu. Each wife has a hut of her own in which she lives with her children. She lives in a portion of her husband's banana grove near his other wives. Girls are free to choose their own husbands, although their mothers urge them to marry well. If she follows her mother's advice, her husband will be wealthy enough to give her cattle which she will own.

[1] O. J. Raum, *Chagga Childhood*, p. 290f.

Like the Tanala, the Chagga count their wealth in cattle. And like the Tanala a man will keep his wealth a closely guarded secret. No one will know his true worth. A wealthy Chagga disperses his cattle among a number of herds to prevent them all from being seized in a single raid and also to keep his stock undetected even by members of his own family.

Unlike the Tanala, the Chagga frequently slaughter cattle, goats, and sheep for their meat. Women tend the fields, gather grass for their cattle, and milk their animals. Women furnish all of the food except for meat which only the men supply. The Chagga also use dung for fertilizer, knowledge the Tanala lacked.

Males are more dominant among the Chagga. Residence is patrilocal, wives moving to their husband's land. Descent is patrilineal: the Chagga pattern is for the eldest son and the youngest son of each wife to inherit the father's lands and herds. As a rule only on his deathbed does a Chagga father reveal the locations of his animals. The women believe that at one time they were dominant and the men seized power through trickery. The same belief is shared by the Kikuyu.

However, among the Chagga an unusual myth is associated with males. Their superiority is assigned to a belief that their anuses are plugged. This secret must be maintained among the men. A man who fails to keep this secret faces the utmost disgrace. Young men are initiated into manhood by circumcision. Preferably all the young men of an age-group will be initiated with the son of a chief. During the circumcision those who have been unruly and disrespectful to their elders are singled out for a painful experience. Taught that flinching at this crucial test of manhood is shameful, the initiates have steeled themselves for the ordeal. For most it is over quickly. But for the mischievous, a deliberate torture awaits. After the circumcision has started, the process is stopped. Someone may stamp on the victim's foot to see if he flinches. He may be required to sing a song as if nothing were amiss. The hazing may last an hour before his foreskin is finally cut completely off. When word of this torture reaches the uninitiated children, it leaves the disobedient shaking with terror at the prospect.

Following this rite, the young men receive information that only male adults share. The males learn that their superiority resides in the anal plug. They are taught:

> Don't emit wind in the presence of women and uninitiated youths. If you do, the tribal elders will slaughter your cows. Beware lest you be surprised by women when you defecate. Always carry a stick with you, dig your feces in, and scratch about here and there, pretending you are digging in some charm. Then if a woman should have observed you, she will seek and find nothing. If you have no stick, tie your feces in the corner of your cloth and throw it away in a safe place. Particular care is necessary after your marriage. When you are seized with gripes, do not tell your wife. If you suffer from looseness of the bowels, call one of your age-mates to take you to the men's house to look after you there. If tapeworm is troubling you, send your mother or an old woman for the male-fern medicine; they know how to keep a secret. For if your bride gets to know about it, it means misery to you! If you dare to tell anybody of the secret of men, your age-groups, the tribal elders and the chief will without mercy deprive you of all you own. For you would have disgraced your contemporaries—yea, the very dead themselves. And it will be said that the secret of the men is a lie![2]

The Chagga in Table IV (p. 81) were rated second only to the Tanala for lack of indulgence in the anal system. Mothers begin very early to train their infants for much the same reason as Tanala women do: soiled clothing is offensive. During the initiation, men are taught to be patient with their wives if a child has soiled their clothing. Men are forbidden to swear at their wives for a child's incontinence. The teaching exists, no doubt, to check a very real impulse on the part of the husband. An abusive husband, in any case, may have to answer to his wife's brother. While men may be

---

[2] Raum, *Chagga*, p. 318f.

superior, Chagga women have their rights. The child who is not responsive to training may be beaten. That toilet training is a source of anxiety for a considerable number of Chagga is suggested by the fact that enuresis is one ground for divorce. Secrecy is not limited to cattle; secrecy extends to food supplies also. Children do not learn the word for meat but are taught a more general word for food lest they inadvertently reveal the family's larder. Gifts of meat are concealed. The calving of a cow, the brewing of beer, the slaughtering of an animal are not for outsiders to know. The Chagga interest in wealth, in secrecy, in the fiction of a stopped anus suggest the aftermath of harsh toilet training.

The oral experience of the Chagga is reminiscent of the Dobu. As on Dobu, only the mother may breast-feed the infant. The Chagga believe that the milk of anyone other than the mother will poison the baby. The threat of sorcerers and witches may lead the parents to bring in a magician to protect the infant. Especially feared is the evil eye which makes the skin peel or kills outright, rupturing the heart. Therefore women feed their infants in secret. Even the sex of an infant is concealed to ward off danger. A mother will not respond to the hailing cry of a visitor. If she does, it is believed her breasts will dry up.

Mother's milk is supplemented by other foods. As early as the second day, bananas, milk, and butter are spat into the infant's mouth. This occurs daily until the third month when the infant may eat any Chagga food except meat. After three months the mother returns to her work. She may be collecting grass for her cattle, tilling the fields, or at a local market selling her surplus. As on Alor, mothers resume their work in the fields, and the small child frequently goes without.

The Chagga infant, with its mixed diet of fattening foods, will tug at its mother's breasts for three years. However this is not a lengthy period of unalloyed oral gratification; its mother after the third month is frequently away for long intervals. Nevertheless the Chagga child received all of the attention of its mother undisturbed by its father until it was weaned.

It is the custom in many African cultures with polygamous families for the mother with a newborn infant to forego copulation with her husband during lactation. Among the Chagga the postpartum taboo on intercourse is three years. Her cowives will occupy her husband while she nurses her child. In some parts of Africa women are thought to resent childbirth because the lengthy postpartum restriction on intercourse denies them their husband's attention. Resort to frequent abortions circumvents the custom. O. F. Raum in *Chagga Childhood* reported that women sometimes commit suicide if they become pregnant within the three years they were supposed to be abstaining from intercourse.

Fathers want sons to maintain the lineage, to win recognition from the chief, and to support their mothers. Mothers need children since the child creates the family. Without a child the family is incomplete, and the mother is unfulfilled. In her old age the mother will depend upon her youngest son for her support. For that reason, inheritance among the Chagga is biased in favor of the youngest son over the eldest. At the same time, childbirth removes the mother from competition with her cowives for her husband's affection for a fairly long time. And husbands' gifts of meat, slaughtered or on the hoof, are the rewards of successful competition. The secrecy of each mother over her infant and over her food is obviously an attempt to ward off the effects of jealousy among her cowives, who may use witchcraft to injure her. Whatever evil Chagga women see in the eyes of others is probably a projection of their own envy. Like the Dobu, sorcery and witchcraft are harmful only for short distances so those who conspire against each other are near.

During the three-year period, the Chagga mother has considerable cause for an ambivalent reaction to her offspring. For a mother, three children adds up to nine years of sexual abstinence or guilt over transgression. Does the mother's anxiety over anyone else feeding her infant enable her to conceal from herself her own mixed feelings over the infant's arrival? As, for example, in our own society an overprotective mother might unconsciously feel hostility for her unwanted child. In the Chagga mother's circumstances, there is reason to suppose that she both wants and does not want a child. The culture has created in her the necessity of having children to validate her social role. She also needs children for her future security. But the price she pays one way or another is also real. And the infant is the tangible reminder of her dilemma.

This line of reasoning is supported by the uncommon amount of punishment dealt out by mothers to their young. Slapping is commonplace. A mother will slap an infant who refuses food. The Chagga child must learn to take it. Later the boy-child will be taunted by others saying he will succumb to the pain of circumcision, that if he frowns or even moves his big toe he will be beaten. A surly father who has had too much beer may thrash a child. Beating older children with a stick is made even more painful by rubbing salt and fat on the buttocks. A mother, angry over a child's behavior, may hurl it to the ground and with a knife scrape the skin from its legs. Or if a girl has refused to help her mother, her mother will tie a cloth around her head and hang her up on a post until the child relents. Or a child is placed in a bag of nettles or in a bag filled with lizards, mice, and other frightening animals. Sometimes after pinching and beating a child, a mother may suspend it over the fireplace so smoke will be an irritant. Or the mother may stop the child's breathing by holding her hand over its nose and mouth. The child is reduced to trembling terror, its urinary and anal sphincter controls gone. And afterwards, the mother may lavish affection on the infant, licking it or offering it food.

Chagga infanticide is another indication of ambivalence toward children. An infant born to a mother still suckling a child is put to death. So is any infant whose birth was in any way abnormal. One of a pair of twins was always killed. If the twins were a boy and a girl, the mother with all sons would let the girl live; if all her children were girls, the boy would survive. Children who were born with teeth were also killed. A child whose upper teeth appeared before his lower teeth would be put to death, the reason being that this was a sign of future conflict between the father and child.

The mother who bears a child while still suckling another has obviously violated the postpartum taboo on intercourse. The abnormal delivery, thought to be ominous for the child's future, may be the eugenics of a herding people familiar with the difficulties of defective animals. Killing one of a pair of twins is paradoxical. The Masai, from whom the Chagga learned much and were in many ways thought to imitate, rejoiced at the birth of twins. The Chagga had more food than the Masai. Perhaps the explanation lies in the belief that a mother's milk was seldom adequate for her child. Other foods were a necessary supplement to prepare the infant for the mother's early departure when she returned to her work. However, other foods could as easily serve the needs of twins. Recently, research has indicated that a mother who is reluctant to nurse her offspring produces less milk than the mother who eagerly anticipates nursing. The inadequacy of the Chagga mother's milk for even a single child may be, in part, the result of her ambivalence toward her child from the start. And killing a child who cut his upper teeth before his lower seems like just an excuse to terminate the obligations of motherhood. To give as a reason the future conflict of father and child suggests in Freudian fashion the very real existence of a conflict in the present over the needs of the father and the needs of the child where both have their locus in the ambivalence of the mother.

In this context the initiation of Chagga women is relevant. In Africa, genital operations are frequent for both sexes. Africa is so large and varied in cultural practices it is very difficult to generalize. If this is true of the Indian in North America, it is even more true of the African. The Kipsigis, Gusii, and Kuria in Kenya have genital operations for both sexes; the Logoli have them for boys but not girls. The Kikuyu near Mount Kenya practice both male and female circumcision; the neighboring Luo practice neither. When the British arrived in Kenya, they naturally found female circumcision among the Kikuyu abhorrent and tried to suppress it. Wokabi Murage, a native Kikuyu, told me that the outcry of the elders was loud and long until the British recognized tribal prerogatives.

The Chagga have both. The time and circumstances surrounding genital operations in each culture vary also. For Chagga girls, the clitoris and labia majora are cut away as part of a group initiation just prior to their first menstruation. The flesh is buried at the foot of a banana tree whose fruit no child may eat. The association between clitoridectomy and denial of food to children fits the thesis being outlined here. More to the point is that most girls are married not long after the operation, and a major consequence of the operation is that childbirth is made excruciatingly painful as a result of the scarification in the genital area. The effect, then, is a deterrent to having many children and a further emotional complication attending each infant's arrival.

When the infant is born, midwives attend the mother and, if deemed necessary by Chagga custom, drown the baby in a pot of water. Exceptions saved some. A breech birth was allowed to live if a firstborn. Girls were not killed despite the early appearance of teeth, but the guilty secret had to be kept. Often, instead of killing the baby, it was simply neglected and died of parental indifference. This was often the case with twins. The delay sometimes saved a child who won parental affection or whose abnormality was outgrown.

The husband's mother directs the midwives while the wife's mother watches anxiously in the background. The wife has been taught that her crying will kill the baby. Her courage will enhance the pride of all women; she knows her husband is listening outside. At the moment of birth, a cry of victory will rise up from the women, the same cry that follows a successful hunt or raid. The husband's mother will lick the baby clean. The husband, upon hearing the baby's first cry, spits toward the sky and enters his grove to prepare a sacrifice for his ancestors.

Spitting is a frequent Chagga custom. For the father, spitting toward the sky is an appeal to his ancestors. Children learn to spit at the age of one, and spitting at each other is a game. Later, boys compete to see who can spit farthest. Adults spit as often as their saliva permits, but no angry male would spit at his father. Such a sin requires a sacrifice. Otherwise no one is ever discouraged from spitting. Remember that from earliest infancy food is spat into the child's mouth. It is as if he spends his lifetime spitting back. In many other cultures as well, an infant's nose is pinched, and with her other hand, the mother forces a thin gruel into the child's mouth when he opens it to breathe. It would be interesting to discover if in such cultures choking or suffocation is frequent among adults.

The role of the father's mother during childbirth anticipates the time when the child is weaned. The Chagga often wean a child by sending it to live with grandparents. The firstborn is sent to the father's parents, the second to the mother's parents. Sometimes the children stay with their grandparents one or two years. Sometimes the children return when they are old enough to tend the goats. Some children remain with their grandparents until their marriage. Grandparents are generally indulgent toward the children and later teach them Chagga customs. The grandparents also like to have grandchildren to work for them, preferably girls, who do domestic service. Having many grandchildren is a sign of wealth. For the parents, sending a child to its grandparents acknowledges filial obligations, just as a Chagga man will send his parents the best cut of meat from a slaughtered cow.

For the mother, however, the loss of her child would be distressing unless she had been prepared by an ambivalent attitude toward her offspring which has been postulated in this analysis. There is enough variation in Chagga custom to allow for all degrees of maternal affection. Some children are reared at home. Some leave for a relatively short period. And some never return.

How do the children respond to the circumstances of their rearing? Are there sufficient grounds to reasonably suppose that a host of hostile impulses linger long after childhood events have been "forgotten"? Is there a target for much of this hostility, or is it displaced into other channels? Is suicide or excessive consumption of alcoholic beverages frequent? Are there cultural patterns, "secondary institutions," which express or release repressed aggression?

Warfare could be singled out as adaptive in Chagga culture. The Chagga won many a battle against the Masai. Chagga heroes like Horombo and Mangi Sina exemplify Chagga courage and skill as warriors. The shaming of cowards by women in the marketplace, the trading of ivory and slaves for Arab muskets, the stone forts held on hillsides against attack—these and more were part of the military life that gave so much importance to Chagga chiefs.

But I would like to suggest another "secondary institution!" The Chagga home has been called a mother-child household because the father is a transient member. Mother takes on most of the responsibility for disciplining the children. She communicates her envy and resentment toward more favored wives to her sons who thereby come to resent their half brothers. Witchcraft is thought to be far more common among the women. Women both create and receive aggression. The practice of clitoridectomy is, in part, an institutionalized expression of aggression toward women, who create and become the target for considerable animosity.

At least it seems to me that this interpretation is in the Kardiner tradition. The practice is functional within the pattern of Chagga culture, and at the same time such an outrage is the disguised expression of childhood rage striking back at mothers with unerring aim. If the circumcision of the male is the occasion for settling accounts with unruly male malefactors, the genital operation on the female balances other accounts. Ethnocentrism aside, why should one be any more shocking than the other? Or have different aims? Or have different motives?

In Chapter 4, the Comanche were rated among the most indulgent of the seventy-five cultures in the Whiting and Child sample whether we consider five systems of behavior or Freud's three. Yet the Comanche valued warriors and guerrilla raids above all else. Here is a culture where child-rearing patterns not conducive to the formation of aggressive impulses are found side by side with adult behavior and values in direct contradiction to the Kardinerian model.

The explanation of this apparent anomaly is historical.[3] The lack of integration between child rearing and adult values represents a late cultural adaptation to new alternatives, the horse and the gun, both brought by transplanted Europeans.

Before the Comanche became renowned warriors, they were a group of bands living in the Montana plateau between the Rocky Mountains and the coastal ranges bordering the Pacific. They spoke a Shoshonean language and like other Shoshone bands without agriculture or domesticated animals, they lived a hand-to-mouth, catch-as-catch-can existence. They dug for roots, foraged for nuts, and

---

[3] Abram Kardiner et al., *The Psychological Frontiers of Society*, pp. 81ff.

hunted antelope, deer, and small game. Camps were moved frequently as food became scarce where they were, and edible seeds and fruits could be gathered elsewhere. Women carried their few possessions from place to place when the elders, who were respected for their knowledge of the territory, recommended moving to a new area.

Fraternal wife-lending and probable infanticide suggest that food was often scarce. Marriage and divorce were not accompanied by an exchange of property. No chief or clans existed. Only small migratory groups, constantly on the move, leaving their temporary brush shelters behind, were able to survive under these demanding economic conditions.

For thousands of years, small bands of Comanche wrested a marginal living from this arid plateau region. And during this long period, they were not known to war upon each other. They lacked the complex social organization that makes war possible. They also lacked anything worth fighting over. They themselves were raided for slaves by more aggressive neighboring tribes; their response was to flee for their lives. The Comanche for most of their history were a peaceful people.

Finally, for unknown reasons they migrated to western Texas, arriving between 1680 and 1690. Whatever the reasons—a failure in the food supply or a final escape from hostile neighbors—the Comanche could not have chosen a more auspicious moment for their own future.

At Santa Fe, New Mexico, the Spanish had established an outpost where wool, fruit, and vegetables were abundant. In 1540 when Coronado arrived in the region, he did not find gold, but he did find the agricultural communities of the Pueblo Indians along the Rio Grande. In 1598, the Spanish sent a large expedition of soldiers, priests, and settlers to colonize the region. By 1610 they had enslaved the Indians, and Indian labor produced the rich harvests that supported the provincial capital at Santa Fe. During this period, death was the penalty for any Indian discovered astride a horse. In

1680, for the only time in recorded history, the Pueblo Indians united in a revolt that killed more than four hundred Spaniards and drove the Spanish from the territory.

It was at this time that the Navaho acquired their sheep; and more important for Indians throughout the Plains and the West, horses were now in the hands of Indians to begin the transformation of Indian cultures.

It was at this propitious moment that the Comanche arrived in the region. And as it did with so many others, the horse revolutionized Comanche culture. Their new mobility made possible more effective hunting, and an increased food supply supported a larger population. Their location, between the Spanish who returned to reconquer the Pueblos and reestablish themselves in Santa Fe in 1692 and the French colonies to the east and the English to the north and east, provided continuous opportunities to raid from one to trade to the other. The Comanche raided for horses which they would then trade for guns; or raided for cattle which they traded for horses; or raided neighboring Indian tribes for slaves—anything that could be captured and exchanged.

The Comanche warrior who led raiding parties became the most prestigious figure in a Comanche camp, the war chief. From small bands of meek men scrabbling for survival over thousands of years, the Comanche became, in two short centuries before they were forcibly retired from the field, the most feared "racketeers" in the Southwest.

More than anything else, the horse changed their culture. When we have used the automobile for two hundred years, social scientists of the future will probably attribute as much change in our culture as the horse brought the Comanche.

The elders who formerly were respected for their knowledge were given, in the altered pattern of Comanche culture, the honorary title of peace chiefs but exercised no real authority at all. The young commonly mocked the elders. Embittered older men were often killed by young men who blamed illness and death upon the "bad medicine" used by the old against the young. In the Plateau culture, the medicine man was the most powerful figure in the group; in the new pattern he was often victimized by the more powerful young.

Contact with European culture, particularly the borrowed elements of the horse and gun, effected many changes, but change has never been total. Many beliefs and values persisted. Some facets of a culture are more resistant to change than others. Child rearing has generally been considered more resistant to change than, say, clothing or cooking. The indulgent child-rearing practices of the Comanche probably persisted relatively unchanged from the earlier Plateau culture when the Comanche thought of themselves as a harmless people. The indulgence of aggressive behavior is consistent with the new pattern, but the indulgence of other systems very likely persisted from the earlier period so that in their warrior period, which was comparatively brief, there was a lack of integration between many child-rearing practices and the cultural expectation that every boy would become a warrior.

6. Nonaggressive Cultures

In this chapter we have at last come to a contrasting group of cultures where the expression of aggressive impulses is at a minimum. In general, expect to find that the frustration-aggression hypothesis holds. Its application here suggests that the accumulated frustrations of childhood provide the reservoir of aggressive impulses which are bodied forth in the cultural patterns of a particular society. Not only in warfare but in all ways the hate-full can release their hate, because our goal is not an understanding only of aggression but of hatred and of human evil.

The frustrations associated with basic drives like hunger, elimination, and, later, sex are paralleled by Freud's emphasis on the significance of oral, anal, and Oedipal experiences. The guiding hypothesis of this inquiry has been that the impact of any culture's style of child rearing is such that the earliest frustrations, those surrounding feeding, create more aggressive impulses than later frustrations, those involving toilet training or the thwarting of sexual impulses; but that it is not the frustration of any single system in the Whiting and Child sense; but by a kind of psychological summation the accretion of layer upon layer of residual fury that burns inside each individual as a result of the total process accounting for and providing the impulse base for culturally defined expressions of human aggression. In the cultures described in this chapter, those fires burn low.

We shall begin with the Siriono, who stood out in the Whiting and Child sample for their high initial satisfaction potential and low socialization anxiety.[1] The food quest dominates the lives of the Siriono. Hunting and gathering in the tropical forests of eastern Bolivia, the Siriono understand hunger. What agriculture they know is limited to burning over a small patch to plant corn, manioc, camotes, cotton, and tobacco with digging sticks. With no techniques for the preservation of food except hanging up live tortoises, hunger drives the Siriono almost continuously in the search for sustenance.

Without even the dog for companionship and help, the Siriono stalks his game with bow and arrow, the longest bows and arrows known. Bows average eight feet long and arrows, nine feet. The Siriono consider shorter bows inferior. The skillful hunter is easily the most important person in Siriono society. With gifts of food, he attracts wives to surround his hammock where he can be found until his most recent catch is eaten. Then he leaves in search of tapir, wild pig, monkey, bird, crocodile, coati, armadillo, puma, or the feared jaguar.

If he returns with meat, it will be distributed within his family only. He will get the back of the animal, and his first wife will take the two hind legs. The rest is divided at random and is usually consumed at a single sitting, nothing being left for envious onlookers. If he returns empty-handed, he will be ridiculed, and his family will go hungry.

The Eskimo also hunts for his survival, but he has one advantage: he lives in a natural refrigerator. He also knows how to make fire with the bow drill. The Siriono have forgotten how to start a fire. If the fire goes out, hot coals must be borrowed from another fire for the Siriono will not eat raw meat. On the march, the hot coals are carried from site to site as the Siriono move in small bands into new territory where both men and women will gather edible nuts and wild fruits, and the men will renew the hunt.

[1] Allan Holmberg, *Nomads of the Long Bow.*

We all have an image of the Eskimo bundled up against the cold, warm in his furry skins. The aboriginal Siriono in a tropical climate wears next to nothing: a necklace or red body paint, an armband colored by the red dye made from urucu seeds or just a beard, or a few feathers glued into the hair with beeswax.

Like the Eskimo and like the Comanche in the Montana Plateau region before European contact, the Siriono are not warriors. Like the Comanche, they were raided by hostile neighboring tribes, and their response was to flee to more inaccessible regions.

And like the Comanche, the Siriono are very indulgent in their child rearing. Babies are a source of status to their mothers. Infants are given the breast freely. Weaning is late and gradual; small children are never fully weaned until they are at least three. Children are loved and are never beaten. The strict toilet training of the Tanala, so careful that their clothing is not soiled, finds no parallel among the Siriono who wear no clothes at all. A Siriono mother is simply indifferent to her infant's urine trickling down her leg. It can be easily washed off; she is never far from water. Even adult Siriono display a casual attitude toward elimination. Feces are deposited just outside their living quarters which consists of one large structure roofed with leaves and housing all members of the band. When the smell becomes unbearable, they move on.

The sex drive among the Siriono is seldom frustrated. A virile male who is a good hunter will have a number of wives. However, as in most societies, most men find one wife all they can support. Still, all men have sexual access to their wife's or wives' sisters and to all potential spouses who are defined as their mothers' brothers' daughters (cousins). Similarly all wives have access to their husbands' brothers and potential husbands, their fathers' sisters' sons. This comparative sexual freedom is reflected in their attitude toward their children's sexual impulses. Inhibiting them is just not a matter of any great significance.

Even a child's aggressive impulses are not inhibited. The child who assaults his parents is laughed at in return. He may even be encouraged to vent his anger in this way as one sign that as an adult he will be strong, courageous and a good hunter.

However, despite this uncommon degree of indulgence that made the Siriono stand out in the Whiting and Child sample, there is one feature of Siriono childhood that cannot be overlooked. The Siriono favor a hairstyle with a high, hairless forehead. And since Siriono babies are born with a full head of black hair, mothers pull out their infants' hair, including their eyebrows, beginning the day after their birth. This painful process occurs every two weeks throughout childhood. Since Siriono infants are born with a strikingly low hairline, the biweekly agony of the infant constitutes an early, severe, and periodic frustration that undoubtedly has lasting consequences.

Despite the degree of childhood indulgence and the comparative freedom and equality of Siriono adults, their lives are no romantic idyll. Dependent as they are upon the chances of the hunt, suffering the endless annoyance of countless insects, and with their meager material culture paralleled by an equally meager elaboration of their lives in folklore, myth, and legend, these survivors of the Old Stone Age struggle to surmount the harsh conditions of their forest environment.

Aggression among the Siriono takes various forms. Hunting is one way he releases aggression. Each man stalks his quarry at least every other day, and he may or may not bring home food. When he is not hunting, he is repairing his equipment, jealously guarding his catch, or envying the luck of others. Disputes over food are constant, and many a man takes up his bow and arrow in anger hoping to return in triumph, not that he would ever show it. Wives quarrel over a fair distribution of food. At night, men dream of tomorrow's catch: hunger haunts them night and day.

Whenever enough honey is located, a mead is brewed, and the men hold a drinking bout. If there is enough mead, the men get drunk. Under the influence of alcohol, the men shout insults at each other, and wrestle until they fall to the ground in a drunken stupor. Fist fighting learned from the white man is discouraged.

Another form of aggression is bloodletting. Adult men and women, after they have had children, have their arms punctured by the dorsal spine of a stingray to get rid of old blood and to rejuvenate them. One of their very few ceremonial observances, this rite is held once a year and is accompanied by drinking brewed mead. A feast also occurs but everyone eats at his own fire, unaccustomed as they are to sharing food.

The only other form of aggression is one that they share with the Eskimo. If the old cannot keep up when it is time to move, they are left to die alone. How strange that the Eskimo in the frozen North have this trait in common with the Siriono who live in a tropical forest! The explanation seems to be that in both cases the appetite of the elderly outruns their usefulness in an environment where the food supply is limited. But more than that may prompt the Siriono for whom their earliest experiences at the hands of their mothers was the anguish of periodic depilation.

Still, consider the myriad forms of aggression that are absent among the Siriono. Cannibalism is unknown despite real pangs of hunger. Sorcery, a common form of projected hostility, is also absent. The blood feud is absent. Nor is there an elaborate realm of supernaturals who bring illness and death upon them. Nor are murder, theft, and rape found among the Siriono. Neither is there any raiding or open warfare with any of their neighboring bands or tribes.

Some anthropologists would argue that the Eskimo, the

prehistoric Comanche, and the Siriono were all simple band societies lacking the complex social organization that makes institutionalized warfare possible. True. But that is not the point. The point is that there is this remarkable congruence between the amount of aggressive behavior in a society and the amount of frustration incident to the child-rearing patterns of that same society. After all, despite real hardship, occasional drunken brawls are not terribly threatening. And despite the quarreling over food, divorce is rare among the Siriono.

The warfare that is associated with more complex societies such as our own is not a necessary consequence of that complexity. The cultural differentiation makes warfare possible, perhaps even probable; but there is no biological instinct, no tainted evolutionary history that makes violence a part of the natural condition of man. What must be conceded is that systematic aggression paid off. If the Europeans who pre-empted the Americas in the last four centuries had neither the will nor the power to displace the native population, world history would have to be rewritten. Only superior firepower and ordered violence enabled Western man to extend his culture from Hudson Bay to the Straits of Magellan.

In this sense, warfare and the whole catalog of iniquities and virtues identified with European culture enabled Western man to dominate other cultures in every part of the globe, to exterminate some and transform others. But the terrifying prospect is that his very power may prove his undoing, unless he himself is transformed into a less aggressive representative of a less aggressive culture.

Another culture where aggression is notable for its absence is among the Lepchas of Sikkim, who farm the lower slopes of Mount Kinchenjunga in the Himalayas not far from Mount Everest. In 1937 when Geoffrey Gorer observed them in the village of Lingthem, warfare was foreign to their cultural tradition. A cooperative, generous, timid people, aggression among the Lepchas occurs in only three forms, suicide, the nagging wife, and the punished child. A closer look at the Gorer material may reveal how the Lepchas managed to almost eliminate disruptive emotional states like envy, jealousy, and nearly all forms of aggression.

The infertile terraces where the Lepcha grow their crops of dry and wet rice, maize, buckwheat, cardamom, and millet require hard work and help from many hands at harvest time. The consumption of food is the main pleasure in life. Feasts are the major events in their social life. Gifts of food to take home after a feast to be eaten later are commonplace. Generosity, especially with food, and working harmoniously together in their fields are two outstanding qualities of the Lepchas. Even children will say they know their parents love them because they give them food. Getting and sharing food dominates their activities as the Lepcha family dominates their lives.

The Lepcha family is an extended, patrilineal, patrilocal family where the oldest male in the prime of life has the most authority. Marriages are arranged by an uncle or someone other than the parents, who play no formal role in the marriage apart from financing the exchanges that are part of the ceremony. Differences between the sexes are minimized: the only things a Lepcha woman cannot do that a male can is kill an animal, own land, or perform certain religious ceremonies. Each wife enters a new home in a new village since each village is made up of exogamous clans. This transition to a strange husband in a strange village is often the most frightening experience in a young girl's life. However, after the marriage she is able to visit her parents as often as she wishes, and her children are likely to marry back into her parents' village.

Lepchas practice polygamy and fraternal polyandry. If a man's first wife is sterile, he is allowed to take a second. A man may also inherit his deceased older brother's wife, and a widower has a claim for a wife from his dead wife's clan, preferably a younger sister of hers. More rare is the marriage form where a man invites his younger brother to become a cohusband and share his work and his wife.

Lepcha attitudes toward sexuality tend to reduce any conflict arising from strong emotional attachment between individuals. After her marriage a wife may be inherited at some future time by any of her husband's younger brothers, any of the sons of her husband's uncles, and any of her older sister's husbands. A wife is free to grant sexual access to any or all of these potential spouses. Similarly, her husband may inherit any of the wives of his older brothers, the wives of his uncles who are younger than his parents but older than himself, and all the younger sisters of his wife. A husband has sexual access to any or all of his potential spouses. The Lepcha attitude toward sexuality resembles their attitude toward food: it is necessary and available so there is nothing to get concerned about. Lepchas have no word for jealousy. Nor is there any anxiety about the paternity of a child: the wife's husband is assumed to be the father unless absent for a prolonged period.

During menstruation, when males avoid their wives, each wife dreams of intercourse with a spirit who visits women expressly for this purpose. Not to have this dream each month means that the woman will soon die, and the expectation is that this dream, like sexuality itself, will continue for a lifetime.

Despite their more than ample sexual opportunity, the experience has been de-emotionalized in Lepcha culture to reduce conflicts, and the Lepchas reveal and release emotional tension in their continual verbal allusions to sexuality. In any mixed group for any occasion whether a feast, a marriage ceremony, or a ceremony to cure an illness, no opportunity is missed for injecting a reference to sexual experience, directly or indirectly. A flair for suggesting sexuality by clever phrasing or accenting a comic incident evokes gales of appreciative laughter.

Such humor is avoided with relatives whose relationship demands respect. One's parents-in-law rank above all others where delicate treatment is required. The most edgy are the wife and her husband's father, and the husband and his wife's mother although obviously in a patrilocal family this tension falls vastly more often on the wife. However, just after a man is married, he must work for his parents-in-law about half his time. And at this time he is unmercifully teased by his wife's male relatives. For him to reply in kind would be shameful.

And to a Lepcha, shame brings a pain in the belly, the center of their emotional life. Sins like killing an animal are emotionally insignificant, but to be shamed publicly is the strongest and worst emotion a Lepcha feels. One must be careful in his speech because to shame another may provoke his suicide, a too frequent occurrence, but even more frequent are the deliberately unsuccessful attempts at suicide to convey one's innocence of shameful charges.

Shame acts as a powerful agent of social control. Quarreling is shameful, being selfish or lazy is shameful, stealing is shameful. The Lepcha grows up to be sensitive to the social approval or disapproval of the members of his extended family which is later generalized to his village neighbors. He moves within a narrow orbit of conformity for in risking social disapproval, he risks his all. In a culture where shame is the intense center of emotional life, one would not lightly say, "You should be ashamed of yourself."

Freud considered suicide to be self-directed aggression. Lepchas have blocked external expression of aggression and become their own victims. Lepchas do admit that a man may have a bad temper, but in such cases the only acceptable aggression is breaking any of his own property or hacking at a piece of wood with his knife. Apart from these few ways to displace aggression, the anger which is denied when one is shamed is turned against the self and suicide may follow or, more likely, a failed attempt. The Lepchas' "pain in the belly" suggests the real rise in stomach acidity during anger which if prolonged will lead to an ulcer that would be painful.

Lepcha culture also includes a realm of supernaturals that fits Kardiner's analysis of secondary institutions rather impressively. The Lepchas account for all forms of ill fortune as the influence of spirits or devils. Their spirits are both benevolent and malevolent, but all are potentially dangerous and prayers urge both to "go away." Over thirty devils threaten them. One kind accounts for envy, another for death, another for evil thoughts. The quarrel devil is a trinity: three devils in one causing enmity of speech, thought, and act. Most are for illness, including the fever-devil, a devil of heart pain, eyeache, skin disease. The Lepcha are not amused when someone says, "The devil made me do it."

Two groups of religious specialists deal with spirits— Lamas and Mun. In dealing with devils, the Lepcha pay a Mun to conduct the appropriate ceremony and frequently make sacrificial offerings. Lamas also cast horoscopes to foretell any harm that might come if the proper precautions are not taken. Both the Mun and the Lamas protect them from imminent danger from frightening spirits.

If Kardiner is correct, Lepcha spirits are disguised projections of infantile anxiety aroused during developmental crises. An infant is fed its mother's milk whenever it cries and is always allowed to suckle until it loses interest. The birth of another baby after three or four years signals the weaning of an earlier child. The youngest child is permitted to suckle until the mother's milk dries up or it "becomes ashamed" which may be as late as puberty. The Lepcha believe mothers never stop lactating. Gorer witnessed a grandmother suckling an infant even though over twenty years had passed since she had given birth and from his observations concluded that Lepcha women lactate much more easily than European women.[2] In addition to such uninterrupted oral gratification as nursing, a Lepcha mother will occasionally play with her baby's lips and tongue with her tongue. When nursing is finally disrupted by a newborn, the older child is told the baby is a devil the size of a small child who brooks no rivalry.

Unlike Lepcha liberality in breast-feeding, parents begin training in elimination as early as three months. Periodically the baby is carried to the balcony which edges the north and east sides of most houses. Parents encourage babies to cry on internal cues and, when they are able, to crawl to the balcony themselves. If a child soils another family member's property, severe punishment befalls the child. Since soiling must be fairly frequent with such early efforts at training and since Lepcha houses have only two rooms, one for ceremonial occasions or honored guests and one for all other purposes, it is difficult for a young mother to prevent her infant from voiding on her respected in-laws' belongings.

Gorer thought toilet training was of little emotional significance to parents who would ignore a stubborn child as long as he did not dirty others' things, but there are clues that suggest the impact of the training had far more importance for the child.[3] As with the Tanala, the Lepchas are secretive about their wealth. Gorer found the Lepchas would freely discuss any other subject; any information on wealth Gorer obtained from neighboring villagers. He also discovered that more than anything else, a Lepcha wishes to be rich. And interestingly, after a sacrifice has been offered to the gods, the Lepchas will divide up the meat of the goat or ox and will reclaim any valuables that were part of the offering. Judging by the Tanala and Chagga, severe toilet

---

[2] Geoffrey Gorer, *Himalayan Village*, p. 293.
[3] Gorer, *Himalayan Village*, p. 295.

training is associated with the pursuit of wealth. This indirect evidence leads me to believe that Lepcha anal training is more severe than Gorer supposed. Also it should be mentioned that the Lepcha have anal explanations for illness.

Punishment, along with sphincter control, begins quite early. Another Lepcha attitude increased the occasions for punishing a child. The Lepchas do not have two codes for conduct, one for adults and one for children. All children are treated as little adults and are expected to behave accordingly. A child is considered capable of committing a crime and can be severely beaten. Also the child who annoys his parents or is considered a nuisance will be hit in some way—a rap on the head with knuckles, a switch across the calves, a strike with a stick. A naughty child receives the same treatment. Being naughty is being unfriendly or uncooperative, hitting people, or throwing stones at them, or quarreling. Mothers punish most and always punish immediately after the offense as if they had independently discovered operant conditioning.

Punishing your child is one way to displace aggressive impulses. Another is to nag your husband. Both probably result from the subservient position of the wife in a household where her mother-in-law directs her domestic activities and where she must maintain an attitude of extreme respect toward both her mother- and father-in-law.

The socialization of sexual impulses arouses less cause for frustration. Children witness copulation and childbirth. Small children may be seen imitating copulation at four or five. Girls are married from eight onwards and boys from twelve. Unmarried boys go night crawling at a girl's invitation. Most boys are introduced to adult sexuality at the invitation to sleep with an elder brother's wife or the wife of an uncle. Lepchas frequently sleep with women twice their age and prefer older women in marriage if given the choice. Women ignore menopause and expect a full sexual life from eight to eighty. Any extra attention from a man is interpreted by women as an attempt at seduction. There is no impotence. Sexual behavior is a casual encounter around which it would be dangerous to center one's emotions.

There appears, then, to be no crises associated with Lepcha oral or sexual child-rearing traditions. However, their anal training is more severe. Gorer does refer to the parents' concern over having their clothing soiled, which again is suggestive of the Tanala. Here is the developmental crisis to support Kardiner's thesis. Here is the source of the aggressive impulses which later are so thoroughly controlled by their social norms that they can only be turned back upon the self or projected onto an elaborate body of hostile supernaturals against whom the Lepchas require the double protection of two priesthoods.

Another culture which has fascinated anthropologists is that of the Hopi Indians of Arizona. Known as a peaceful people, the Hopis fought only defensive wars to guard their homes, fields, and water supply from marauding Navaho, Apache, and Ute, especially after they acquired horses from the Spaniards. In self-defense they finally moved from the base of the three mesas where their homes were nearer their crops to the mesa tops where attacking Indians could be seen from great distances and where a very limited access could be easily defended. In fact, since the pueblo uprising of 1680 when the Spanish missionaries were killed or driven out, the Hopis have never been conquered by force of arms.

Occupying a desert region where the annual rainfall is a scant ten to eighteen inches, the Hopis are dependent upon springs that trickle from the southern edge of the Black Mesa. Their stone villages are huddled together on three rocky promontories that jut out from Black Mesa into the Painted Desert and are named according to the order of their discovery from east to west as First Mesa, Second Mesa, and Third Mesa. Oraibi, the oldest settlement and farthest removed from white contact, is atop Third Mesa. Today it is called Old Oraibi because at the bottom of Third Mesa the village of New Oraibi represents a progressive faction that favors accommodation with white culture.

Actually Old Oraibi is nearly abandoned. Earlier, Old Oraibi was the most populated village with about twelve hundred Hopis. But the first division occurred abruptly when a group at Old Oraibi known as "Friendlies," who were more cooperative with whites, had a conflict with the more conservative "Hostiles." They settled their dispute in 1906 with a pushing contest in which the Friendlies literally shoved the Hostiles out of the village by pushing them across a line drawn in the sand just outside Old Oraibi. The more conservative Hopi took their belongings and established the new village of Hotavilla west of Old Oraibi. Further depletion followed when some members of Old Oraibi moved to Moencopi fifty miles west where flood farming made for more abundant crops. Finally, the gradual growth of New Oraibi where Christians and the friendliest of the Friendlies live has reduced Old Oraibi to the appearance of a ruin.

Old Oraibi prefigured succeeding separations that are part of Hopi adaptation to white culture. Throughout Hopiland, division between the traditionalists and the progressives continue as more and more Hopis move down from the Mesas. Moencopi, though not established on a mesa, has divided into upper and lower Moencopi. Upper Moencopi is nearer the Navaho Tuba City and is more progressive.

The arrival of white culture apparently served to release a latent hostility submerged within the traditional Hopi way. What was the Hopi way? How did aggression arise among the Hopi, whose name means "peace"? And how was aggression channeled within the Hopi way?

Farming the desert around them, the Hopis were dependent upon the sun, the rain, and the fruit of both, the sacred corn. Corn was their life. Their bodies were made of the corn they had eaten. The Corn Mother and Mother Earth both respond to the Sun Father when he brings rain.

Cornmeal is used to bless participants in all ceremonies. Two small perfect ears are placed beside a newborn infant. At his death, his hands are filled with cornmeal and his fingers tied together. Meal is sprinkled over his body and rubbed over his face. Cornmeal is sprinkled at the bottom of his grave where in a squatting position he faces east, the direction of life from which the Sun Father first appears. Before the grave is sealed, cornmeal is once more sprinkled over the body, and three days later a path of cornmeal points eastward.

Between birth and death, the Corn-eaters, as the Navaho called them, survived through the centuries because of their tenacious cultivation of scattered patches of corn. Sand, whipped up by an evil wind, shredded or buried their crops. Periodic drought taught them to store a one-to-three-year surplus against starvation. Almost all ceremonies are directly or indirectly a prayer for rain.

Despite the impoverishment of a desert environment, Hopis created an instrumentality without which their survival would have been doubtful: their tightly knit social organization. A Hopi village is made up of resident clans. The village chief is a member of the Bear Clan since the Bear Clan was the first to settle in Hopiland. Certain clans are related so that groups of clans, known as phratries, assist each other in their ceremonies. One must marry outside his phratry. These exogamous clans thus are linked through intermarriage, reducing hostility among the clans, and fostering a common physical identity among the clans who came together originally at different times from different regions.

Hopi families are monogamous, matrilineal, and matrilocal; that is, they have one husband and one wife, inherit from the wife, and live in her house. Obligations to the clan outrank individual desires. Clan members are descended from a common ancestress. The head of the clan, the clan mother, with her daughters and their husbands make up the extended Hopi family. Hopi wives own their homes, all of the food and seeds in them, and most important, own the clan springs and the clan lands which the men work. A Hopi husband belongs to his mother's clan and will return to her home for the ceremonial life of his clan. The male owns his own livestock, fruit trees, personal belongings, tools, and items essential to his ceremonial roles.

Each lineage within a clan has a clan mother, but the leading lineage living in the ancestral house has the real clan mother. Her brother is the ceremonial leader of the clan. Men bring rain and rich harvests only through ritually perfect ceremonial observances: the survival of the tribe rests in their hands and in the hands of their gods.

The wife patiently grinds corn, cooks, makes baskets and pottery, and carries water endlessly up the mesa. She also raises their children who belong to her clan. Her husband herds, hunts, and carries fuel endlessly up the mesa. He also works like a slave to the fields. Together the Hopi wife and her husband follow the Hopi Road of Life, a journey from birth to death to rebirth in the underworld from which all men arise and will return.

The Hopis are now in the Fourth World, three others having been destroyed through the weaknesses of man with three more worlds to come. The Road of Life has carried the Hopi, the chosen people, to their present condition where their strength and wisdom are being tested. Only following the Hopi way can save them from destruction; any other way is "ka-hopi," not Hopi. The Hopi must keep a good heart, free of evil wishes and destructive emotions. With a good heart, one will live long in good health and die peacefully in his sleep. Is there a better wish anywhere?

To maintain their purity, the Hopi follow an annual ceremonial calendar of nine elaborate rituals that are extraordinary religious phenomena. The Hopis' spiritual development rivals any other in the world. I would particularly recommend Frank Waters' *Book of the Hopi* to get a sense of the way the totality of their lives is inspired by religious belief and integrated into a drama of cosmic proportions.

There is probably no better illustration of Malinowski's theory of functionalism in anthropology than Hopi spirituality. In studying the Trobriand Islanders off the coast of New Guinea with whom the Dobu traded, Malinowski described Trobriand culture as a web of complementary institutions, each supporting the other. The concept of culture as a pattern of integrated institutions added a new dimension to the understanding of man and his social life. Malinowski enabled anthropologists to put together the countless specific items they had catalogued into more meaningful relationships.

Applied to Hopi ceremonialism, a functionalist interpretation clarified Hopi belief and practice. Long ago the "kachinas," Hopi gods, came from their homes in the San Francisco Mountains near Flagstaff and helped the Hopi during a time of troubles. Now Hopi men impersonate the kachinas in ritual dances and secret ceremonies. The dances are public and put on by the men of a clan. New songs and dance steps are often required, and the men spend many hours practicing in the men's house, the "kiva."

The kiva is an underground room entered by a ladder from above. A small hole in the floor, the sipapu, is symbolic of the Place of Emergence from the underworld. Each clan has its own kiva. Old Oraibi has fourteen kivas. Each clan owns a special ceremony, and the secret rites are restricted to men who have been initiated into full membership. The kiva is also a men's social club and meeting place, apart from its religious functions.

The major ceremonies last nine to twenty days and are the only diversions in a year otherwise devoted to hard work. The ceremonial year begins with the Wuwuchin in November and ends with the Niman ceremony in July. In the Wuwuchin all fires are extinguished, and the chief priest creates the "New Fire" which relights all homes and kivas. Wuwuchin also marks the initiation of young men into full adulthood. Wuwuchin is followed by the Soyal ceremony when the kachinas arrive in the village. Their main purpose is to turn the sun at the time of the winter solstice signaling rebirth and new life. In February the Powamu ceremony celebrates germination and growth of the crops. It is also the time of the first initiation of boys and girls when they discover to their astonishment that the kachinas are men and not gods. In the Niman ceremony, after which the gods will return to their homes in the San Francisco Mountains, the kachinas give gifts to the children. These gifts are symbolic of the ripening crops that the kachinas created. Their work done for the year, they are going home.

During all of these ceremonies, altars, sand paintings, prayer feathers, and elaborate kachina costumes are prepared in the kivas. Each detail of the ceremony, the songs, and the dances must be practiced until they can be performed with flawless precision or the rain will not come or the crops will fail and the harvest be poor. Each man impersonating a kachina must keep a good heart, free of anger, fear, sadness, or worry; each spectator participates by also keeping a good heart. During and for four days after each ceremony, a participant remains continent.

The Hopi believe their prayers, thought, rituals, and behavior influence the universe. By controlling his thoughts and emotions, by following the proper rituals exactly, by observing the taboos, he participates in nature's harmonious balance. A failure on anyone's part, of act or mind, will bring ruin upon all. Only the resolute pursuit of the Hopi way with one's heart and mind prevents disaster. The arc of the Sun Father overhead, the response of the Corn Mother and Mother Earth, the saving rains, the ripening corn, the fertility of plants, animals, and humans—all depends upon the Hopi way.

Throughout their ceremonial performances—the Snake

Dance, the Flute Ceremony, the Buffalo and the Butterfly dances, the dances of the woman's societies, the humorous antics of the clown kachinas, and those already mentioned— all performers are urged to think rain. Their religious practices are intimately tied to their agricultural necessities. And the internalized discipline required of clan ceremonials and the Hopi way enables the individual Hopi to match the external discipline of farming a desert without irrigation. A closer fit between religious inspiration and economic survival would be hard to discover. Of the Hopi it has been wisely said that without his religion he would have perished.

The Hopi way is not a smooth road. There are not only the hazards of desert farming. It is threatened from within. The greatest perils are presented by the Two Hearts, Hopi who have both a human and an animal heart. Two Hearts bring illness and death. Members of one's own family are suspect. Two Hearts are said to prolong their own lives by the death of a family member. While every adult male participates in the ceremonials and the Hopi have no separate priesthood, they do need medicine men who can remove poisoned arrows that lodge in the bodies of victims, arrows that Two Hearts wing on their evil way.

Taiowa, the Creator, who looks down upon the Hopi through the face of the sun, is the supreme Hopi deity. When he created the first god, Taiowa called him a nephew. Since the mother's brother most often disciplines Hopi children, to think of Taiowa as an uncle reveals an ambivalent attitude toward the Creator who is not solely benign. This same ambivalence is evident toward Masau'u, the god of fire and death, the sight of whom is a warning of death. At the same time, Masau'u guards the village at night and is prayed to as one who can bring rain, increase the population, and help people to live to old age and die without suffering. Even the kachinas who bring gifts and rain are a mixed blessing, sometimes frightening and whipping the children.

The Spider Woman is the best example of an unpredictable Hopi deity. She can capture small children in her web, causing them to die. At the same time, she is revered as the creator of all living things. She has the power to bless all the beings she created; she can bring rain. She guides the Hopi to salt which she owns and is also known as the Salt Woman.

Rocky shrines to Hopi gods dot Hopiland. The Hopi approach their shrines warily with prayer feathers or corn-meal to ask a blessing or see a hopeful sign. Hopi gods can provide blessings, but they are also dangerous.

To the infant, parents are godlike. They may bestow joyous blessings or thunder curses terrifying helpless children. How do the Hopi treat their children? Can we account for their ambivalent gods?

To begin with, the Hopi child is welcome, as one might expect in an agricultural community. Girls are preferred to carry on the lineage. They will stay home and be a comfort to their aging relatives in a society where kinship is very important. But whether boy or girl, a child is a blessing.

The Hopi stress fertility: all of life—the plants, the animals, and the Hopi themselves—depend upon it for survival. Fertility symbols abound in their dances, prayer feathers, and rituals. Sex is not a "sin" to the Hopi; being lazy is.

The first act of the Hopi is symbolic of all Hopi culture: the infant is bound to the cradleboard. The two perfect ears of corn placed one on each side of the infant represent the mother and her infant. The seed of this corn will be planted the following spring. The father's mother binds the infant securely. While the infant is really a member of its mother's clan, it is ceremonially spoken of as the "child" of the father's clan, and his mother offers her services. She has made the cradleboard and supplies the blankets and cotton cloths. She will care for the mother and infant for the first twenty days; thereafter the infant's mother will care for her baby.

Wrapped in the total security of the cradleboard, the infant begins a life that will be tightly circumscribed by the security of the Hopi way where his relationships to all others, his behavior, his thoughts and emotions, his progress on the Hopi Road of Life are all defined within the Hopi customs that evolved under the strenuous conditions imposed by their desert environment.

Some psychologists have seen the cradleboard as a rigid restraint that would enrage the infant. The Hopi use the cradleboard for three months; the infant may be removed from it any time after that. No infants are kept on the cradleboard after six months. A restless or a precocious infant is removed much sooner. Wayne Dennis found that Hopi children bound on the cradleboard walk at the same time as those who were not bound at New Oraibi and Upper Moencopi.[4] He also thought Hopi infants, habituated to the cradleboard from the first day of life, give no evidence of being handicapped in any way by the experience.

The Hopi mother nurses her infant without restraint, stopping only if she becomes pregnant or the child is so old that he is teased by his playmates and stops of his own accord. Don Talayesva, who recounted his life story in *Sun Chief*, continued to run to his mother for milk while he was six years old. Some children suckle until they are seven and eight. Most children are weaned in their second year. Among the Hopi, then, a child is not deprived of oral gratification and the company of his mother who does not work in the fields. In addition, a Hopi child is fed anything he wishes even as an infant and later on is free to eat at any time. There appears to be no frustration of oral needs that would create aggressive impulses.

However, it is again toilet training that differs from the earlier period of unstinting gratification. The first blows fall when the child fails to heed his mother's word to go outside the door. First he is carried out to indicate parental wishes.

---

[4] Wayne Dennis, *The Hopi Child*, p. 107.

When he is able to walk, he is expected to go by himself. Failure brings a scolding or a spanking, and most often from the mother.

While most students of the Hopi consider cleanliness training mild, the indirect evidence suggests otherwise. Like the mother, Spider Woman has creative powers, can be beneficent, but also has a web that, once caught in it, can be fatal. Mother is the source of great blessings, witness the Corn Mother and the Earth Mother, but she is dangerous too. Here again have we not evidence that Kardiner's theory of projection of childhood frustration into secondary institutions is valid?

Most punishment is linked to the mother. When she herself does not punish directly, she calls upon her brother to do so. The child's father very seldom punishes his child. If a child continues to wet his bed at night, the mother's brother will take him along with other boys to the Corn Water clan where cold water will be thrown upon them. The mother's brother will sometimes take a strap to an offending child. The most severe punishment he metes out is the cedar smudge where a child is held under a blanket over smoking twigs until he chokes.

If a choice is possible between punishing a single child or a group of children, the Hopi punish the whole group. The child should learn that his behavior affects all Hopi. A good Hopi works for the good of all. One bad Hopi can destroy everyone's crops. The Hopi way requires unselfish, hardworking individuals who keep a good heart. The Hopi have also institutionalized punishment of children by the use of the So'yoko kachinas and the Powamu initiation. Into the pueblo, banging on doors and calling out for wicked children stalks the So'yoko kachinas. Their leader, note, is a female, So'yo' Kwuti, who carries a meat cleaver to dismember errant children. There is also an "uncle," Tahahum. They enter a house, call out the name of the disobedient child, and threaten to take him away and eat him. A child is sometimes dragged screaming from the house, but most often the parents persuade the kachinas that the child will be good, and then send the kachinas away with gifts of food. Accepting the parent's promises of good behavior on behalf of the child, the kachinas will often leave a gift, say, a bow and arrow, for the boy.

The Powamu initiation ceremony involves whipping the six- to eight-year-old boys. The children are brought into a kiva, stripped, forced to lie down on a sand painting, and whipped individually by Whipper Kachinas. The children are usually given four stripes from long yucca whips supplied by the Whipper Mother, but a miscreant like Don Talayesva was given eight, leaving permanent scars. After the ceremony, the kachinas whip each other and then remove their masks. The children recognize members of their own family. The kachinas, they discover, are not gods but their own relatives and neighbors who imitate the kachinas. Finally, they are warned that if they tell the smaller children what they have seen, they will be more severely whipped and that children have been known to die from such a whipping. No wonder the Hopi are ambivalent toward their gods.

The mother and the maternal uncle, then, in daily life and on more formal occasions, discipline the child beginning with cleanliness training and extending to all of the violations of the Hopi way. As a result Hopi children have temper tantrums and, not surprisingly, Talayesva reports his own attempt at suicide. While I have no data on the frequency of attempted suicide among the Hopi, a little girl seated on the edge of the small saddle that joins Walpi on First Mesa to Hano told me as she looked out over the vast landscape, awesome from that high perch, that her brother had jumped from the spot where she was seated. Where few outlets for aggression are allowed, we have what Freud called the "introversion of the destructive instinct."

Many observers have noted the casual cruelty of Hopi children to small animals, one outlet acceptable to the Hopi. The boys also play a game of war where an attacking group from below storms another group defending a high place.

Among adults, the Hopi are known for their malicious gossip, a form of aggression which serves as the major social control. But the most transparent evidence for Kardiner's position is the belief in the Two Hearts. That witches and sorcerers can inflict illness and death upon others, even on members of their own family, is a rather obvious disguise for aggressive impulses which individuals project toward others. At one point in his autobiography, Don Talayesva even wondered if his mother was a Two Heart.[5]

The institutionalization of aggressive impulses into a form of demonology reveals that peace among the Hopi was a tribal ideal rather than a reality. That Hopi pueblos were not perfectly integrated societies is illustrated by conflicts over clan leadership. Their legends and their history show us brothers disputing each other's claim to leadership roles and whole pueblos splitting up over divided loyalties.

If Kardiner is correct, Hopi culture should reveal in its institutional forms the projected consequences of its child-rearing practices. And if, as hypotheticated here, severe toilet training is the key to Hopi culture, some hint of anal anxiety should reappear in adult institutions. Kardiner pointed specifically to religious beliefs as a common "secondary" institution, and Hopi spirituality provides ample material for analysis. What are the classic Freudian symbols associated with the anal stage in a child's psychosexual development? Excrement is associated with wealth, with gift giving, with perfectionism, and with secrecy.

And what of the Hopi? Where are the secret places? Obviously one is the kiva, where ceremonial equipment is repaired and ceremonies are rehearsed until a perfect per-

[5] L. W. Simmons, *Sun Chief: The Autobiography of a Hopi Indian*, p. 325.

formance, which is the only one that will bring rain, is prepared. And where is the wealth? In a culture where a man owns so little, how can one speak of wealth? Yet there is a wealth, the same wealth that has always strengthened the Hopi for his ordeal in the desert: his spiritual wealth. His ownership extends to the secret rituals of his men's society. His knowledge of the secret rituals which alone bring rain, and so life, to the Hopi is his treasure.

The secret kivas where ceremonial perfection is sought confirm Kardiner's expectations and if more confirmation is required, what do the Hemis kachinas in the Niman ceremony carry with them as they come from the kiva toward the plaza for their ceremonies? The gifts that they will distribute. What a complete and total confirmation of Kardiner's efforts!

Finally, if more evidence is needed, there is one who never punishes, who impregnates the earth, who is life itself, the Sun Father, the face of god. Walking with a father and his son at Hano, I saw a boy beaming with recollected pleasure when he told of the fun he and his father had had the previous winter making snowmen together from the heavy snows that had fallen on First Mesa.

Perhaps it is now clearer whether cultures characterized by a high degree of interpersonal aggression (verbal conflict, fighting, murder, rape), of intrapersonal aggression (severe depressive states, suicide and other self-destructive behavior), and of institutionalized aggression (painful initiation rites, sorcery, infanticide, feuds, raiding, warfare, execution, sacrifice to placate angry spirits) differ markedly from cultures which are less aggressive. Or are the differences slight and insignificant? Put in statistical terms the question is "How large is the variance in the distribution of aggression in the cultures of man?" There is, of course, no way to compute the variance since no one has yet attempted to assign numerical values to the amount of aggression in various cultures.

But we can get some idea of the differences by comparing the ten cultures described in the last four chapters. On a line from least aggressive to most aggressive, a crude approximation would be:

Least Aggressive   *Most Aggressive*

1	2	3	4	5	6	7	8	9	10

- Siriono
- Early Comanche
- Lepcha
- Hopi
- Manus
- Tanala
- Alor
- Chagga
- Marquesan
- Late Comanche
- Dobu

If an attempt were made to guess the distribution of aggression in all the cultures of man, would the distribution be a curve skewed to the left?

This curve assumes that high aggression is a common cultural adaptation among mutually hostile, neighboring

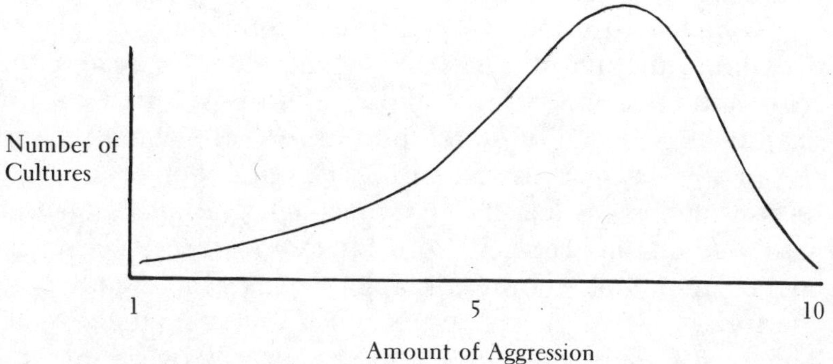

peoples. In the absence of more data, it is also very possibly an ethnocentric projection of our own style of cultural adaptation.

Given our own experience within our own culture, it would be difficult for us to accept a curve skewed to the right.

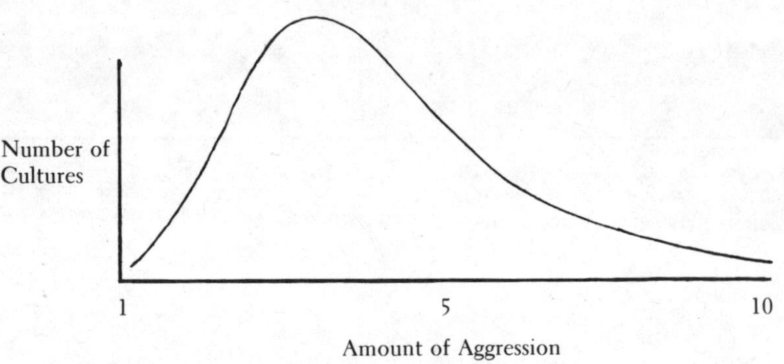

This curve assumes that high aggression is a rare cultural pattern. Actually neither curve may be correct. This inquiry has been limited intentionally to the seventy-five cultures in the Whiting and Child sample and a closer examination of only ten of the seventy-five.

Robert Textor in *A Cross-Cultural Summary* considered over four hundred cultures in an encyclopedic search for cross-cultural relationships among a host of variables. In sorting out the cultures for one aspect of aggression, he classified forty-one as exhibiting extreme bellicosity and forty-six low in bellicosity.[6] Even though one might quarrel with some of his choices, from his examination of a much larger sample of cultures it appears that the number of cultures with high or low aggression is approximately equal. The great bulk of cultures fell intermediate between the two extremes so that the curve may really look like this:

[6] Robert Textor, *Cross-Cultural Summary*, p. 420.

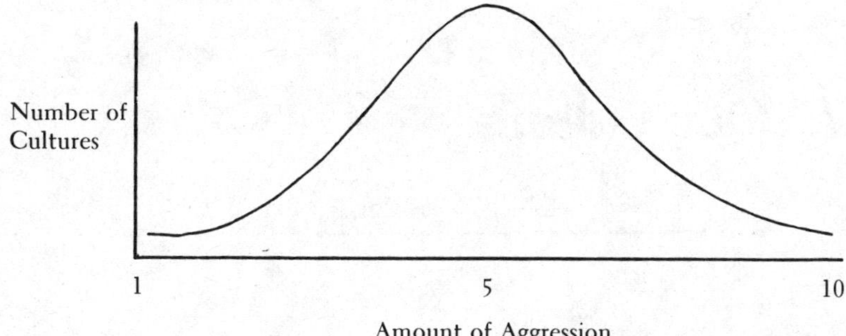

Such a distribution suggests that there is more variation in the cultures of men than can be accounted for by the concept of a universal aggressive instinct.

7. Our Culture

What has all of this to do with us? Just that our culture too is a patterned social organization with a learned tradition that defines beliefs, values, and customary behavior, shaping our daily lives from birth till death and providing the appropriate ceremony for each. But in our case, a complex heterogeneous society, we really have multiple learned traditions with varied beliefs, values, accustomed behavior, and ceremonial alternatives. Still, there is an identifiable, central core that we may call majority culture even if numerous minority variations coexist.

Major features of the majority culture include the monogamous, nuclear family with neolocal residence and bilateral descent; a mixed industrial, herding, and agricultural economy; a Christian religious tradition; and a hierarchy of rule-making organizations whose membership in recent years is periodically changed by a process known as an "election." The tradition includes warfare as an instrument of national policy.

The vast majority of citizens live in and around cities where economic transactions dominate their lives. Great traders, Americans dwell more upon exchange and the wealth called "profit" that accrues from successful exchanges than upon anything else. The people believe that the "profit motive" inspires more behavior than any other motive. A big man in the community, a successful trader displays the material evidence of his achievement for lesser men to envy. So appealing is the prestige attaching to wealth from profitable exchanges that many women imitate men in the pursuit of wealth. And a few resent any barrier to their full participation in exchange activities, even including their own offspring.

The structure of society maximizes competition. An open-class system challenges all to be clever or to work hard to achieve a position of eminence, with certain glaring exceptions. Occupations replace clans as a major source of identity. Within his occupation each man is also occupied with moving up. The most familiar image describing an occupation is the ladder, which one attempts to climb rung by rung until he reaches the top. The openness of the system encourages striving. At the same time, no one can be secure in his position for just one rung away is one's successor. Only continued achievement justifies one's position and proffers a claim to a higher one. While the open-class system produces a degree of anxiety among individuals, it also creates the social conditions for continuous striving for achievement enabling America to produce more than it can properly distribute and making competition one of the central themes in American life.

Competition permeates American culture. Competition for grades in school, for excellence in sports, for promotion at work, for a larger share of the market, for a better profit and loss statement in the annual report, for bigger, better or more of whatever is valued. Both for groups and for individuals, winning brings a special zest. Professional athletics which combines competition and profit making is a good example of American values, providing Americans with their greatest spectacles in huge arenas. The American Christmas is another example where even gift giving becomes competitive and serves to finance retailers and their suppliers throughout the land.

Among men, one card game that epitomizes the American style is poker. A group of friends sit for long hours around a table and try to bluff each other out of their money. Whatever one friend wins, the others lose. A shrewd player sharpens skills in betting, assessing the pretenses or hopes of a competitor, weighing one's chances, exercising restraint, and confusing the competition. All play a part in poker, the friendly game.

Is competition the same as McClelland's need-achievement described in Chapter 1? Individuals with high need-achievement take moderate risks, use feedback to assess progress, and are task-oriented in their fantasies. Their parents expect them to achieve and give them the independence to try. Or is competition a socially approved outlet for aggression? To what extent is the drive to achieve prompted by high need-aggression? Certainly, much competitive behavior looks like sublimated aggression. The cheer goes, "Fight! Fight! Win! Win!" Managers hire aggressive salesmen. Supervisors are urged to exercise aggressive leadership. Often the role of the "boss" or the "chief" enables him to exercise his aggressive drive as well as his need to achieve.

Of the two, I am inclined to see need-aggression as more dominant in social interaction than the more tepid need to achieve. Self-assertion is the surer sign of American character than the earnest effort to get things done. Especially so if one considers the indirect evidence.

Aggression colors all of our social relationships. Violence, hatred, and conflict are as American as apple pie. When clergymen from their pulpits cried out for the meaning of the assassination of President John F. Kennedy in November of 1963, the significance of the act lay all about them. The murders of Robert Kennedy and of Martin Luther King, Jr., further serve to illustrate that while killing in our society is frowned upon, it is not taboo. Taboo behavior in a culture is totally proscribed, so much so that the impulse to engage in tabooed behavior would very seldom enter consciousness.

How often have you thought about another or said outright, "I could kill him!"

These killings of eminent men shock our sensibilities, but they are like the tip of the iceberg. Beneath that tip, we have been loathe to recognize the mammoth body of crime, riots, murders, lynchings, rapes, and suicides that point to a seething hatred that poisons the Western soul. Yes, poisons. How else can one interpret the spirit-shattering horror of the World War II concentration camps, of Hiroshima, of My Lai?

It is not the occasional, highly visible, public affront to our more benign aspirations, but the many more private occasions of family discord followed by divorce or the marriages sustained despite a cordial hatred that reveals the rift between our ideals and our tainted reality. It is the anger burning barely beneath the surface, the chip on the shoulder. Even the common vulgar term for copulation is a swear word used in anger. Truly, it was Freud's insight into the extent of our conflicting impulses that made him an unbridled pessimist.

In recent years studies of personality disturbances in other cultures have been used to gain insight into the patterning of personality. What can we learn about ourselves from our own severely disturbed personalities?

Professionals in the field of mental health do not regard the severely disturbed as different in kind from the normal population, only different in degree. Therefore, although their symptoms are exaggerated, our hospital population magnifies the emotional strains of every man. The lens may be distorted, but the tensions are recognizable because they are so familiar.

The emotionally disturbed are classified under three major categories: personality disorders, neuroses, and psychoses. Personality disorders include drug addicts, alcoholics, sexual deviants, delinquents, and antisocial personalities.

The category includes behavior that is not classifiable as neurotic or psychotic and is at the same time known to be highly resistant to corrective treatment. Neuroses cover a wide range of symptoms with seven major types. Neurotic symptoms range from mild disturbances to fairly severe reactions. Most neurotics do not require hospitalization and have been called the walking wounded. Psychotics usually require twenty-four-hour care and are classified as organic or functional depending on whether there is tissue damage or not. Functional psychoses are believed to be emotional in origin, no physical causation being discoverable.

When an individual can no longer cope, when his defenses are down, does he exhibit the repressed rage that is the fatal flaw in Western character structure? Let's see. Take suicide. Over two hundred thousand Americans attempt suicide each year; about twenty-five thousand succeed in a ratio of three men to each woman.[1] About 35 percent of successful suicides are severely depressed. When severe depression persists, the person is often unremitting in suicidal attempts. The depressed psychotic must be protected from himself. When the ego is vulnerable and powerful aggressive impulses are blocked, a man may victimize himself. In Chapter 2 it was hypothesized that the depression itself was the result of unmanageable aggression.

About 25 percent of first admissions to public mental hospitals represent the functional psychosis called schizophrenia. Recently half of the hospital beds in America were occupied by schizophrenics. Drug therapy may have reduced their numbers, but schizophrenia is still the major challenge to mental health specialists. The schizophrenic has withdrawn from social reality, preoccupied by his own fantasies. His hallucinations tempted doctors to try LSD to get some insight into his mental state. What behavior characterizes schizophrenics? In a study of sixty-four patients with simple

[1] James Coleman, *Abnormal Psychology and Modern Life*, p. 333.

schizophrenia, it was found that fifty-six lacked normal aggressiveness.[2] At the same time, aggressive behavior was their most common symptom: 65 percent of this sample threatened or assaulted others, usually family members, or destroyed property. Almost 43 percent had delusions or hallucinations. Other symptoms were less frequent. The outstanding characteristic in this small sample of one type of schizophrenia was exaggerated aggression. There are nine types of schizophrenia so this one study of one type should not be overemphasized.

Where else is aggression found among the emotionally disabled? The paranoid psychotic has delusions of persecution and of grandeur. Delusions of persecution are very probably projected aggressive impulses. If you imagine everyone is your enemy, where does the enmity lie? In Joseph Heller's *Catch-22*, when Yossarian said everyone was trying to kill him, he linked war with madness by appearing paranoid. Actually, his statement was a literal description of reality gone mad.

The involutional psychotic reaction is marked either by severe depression and the danger of suicide or by paranoid delusions with a tendency to commit acts of violence.[3] Occurring to women between forty and fifty-five and to men between fifty and sixty-five, involutional reactions account for only 4 percent of first admissions to mental hospitals. While many people believe only women suffer the involutional reaction, actually the reaction hospitalizes half as many men as women.

Our most severe mental disturbances, the functional psychoses, which are emotional in origin, include schizophrenia, the manic-depressive reaction, the psychotic depressive, paranoid reactions, and involutional psychotic reactions. All of them reveal to some degree disturbances in normal

[2] Ibid., pp. 276–77.
[3] Coleman, *Abnormal Psychology*, pp. 341–46.

aggressive behavior. Perhaps aggression plays a larger role in the development of psychotic reactions than has been generally recognized. Do not the severely disturbed furnish more evidence on the role of aggression in our culture?

There are other signs too. A popular novel that appeared in recent years, *Lord of the Flies* by William Golding, clearly implies that man is forever fated to die by violence. The children of a Western nation (it appears to be England) are escaping from the dangers of war and are isolated on an island, the pilot of the plane killed. Three boys try to lead the others, all boys. Ralph tries to recreate a democratic society. Piggy's leadership consists of influencing Ralph. Jack, who had a leadership role in a boys' choir, is Ralph's rival.

The three boys mirror Freud's model of the mind. Ralph is the ego. He appeals to reason. He wants to maintain a fire so that they can be rescued. He tries to reconcile the demands of reality with the demands of Piggy who represents the superego and Jack who represents the id. Piggy nags Ralph constantly to do things the right way. Jack becomes the leader of the hunters who will furnish the meat for their diet.

In the competition for the loyalty of the smaller boys, Jack finally wins. Jack organizes them into a tribe with himself as chief. At the end of the book, Piggy's brains are spilled after a fall from a height onto a boulder, and Ralph is running for his life. The ego is in full flight from the raging id.

The book argues that there are dark forces more powerful than reason, forces which will overthrow reason every time, that reason is helpless before the onslaught of the passions. It argues that these isolated children relived and rediscovered this truth revealing the real nature of man.

Such a conclusion is true in the sense that these boys had already been exposed to the formative influences of child-rearing practices in our culture. These children probably are an adequate sample of our culture and their experiences imaginatively representative. Unhappily, Golding's case is plausible, but rather then baring man's nature, it represents our character structure, our style of socialization, the consequences of the ways we raise our children.

The real nature of man is not revealed by *Lord of the Flies*. What is revealed is one rather widespread possibility. Other cultures have nurtured other possibilities. There is no one human nature, only the myriad varieties produced by all of the cultures of history and prehistory.

It must be pointed out that Jack's conception of a tribe is another Western fiction. Real tribes are not marauding savages ruled by an omnipotent chief. This myth is essentially another projection of our own unconscious. Real tribes often invest very little power in the "chief" and are often more humane than we are. Many American Indian tribes, for example, gave very little authority to a single chief. And many tribes accepted whites into full membership in the tribe without discrimination based on color, creed, or national origin.

Another instance of our preoccupation with aggression is the way in which Hollywood ends a Western with the shoot-out between the good guys and the bad guys. As a classic American morality tale, the Western is our equivalent of a folk myth and, as such, reveals American character. Consider Wild Bill Hickok of the thirties. He is in a saloon leaning against the bar with one foot resting on the rail. He wears a white hat and his pearl-handled six-guns gleam in their holsters. In film after film, he keeps repeating, "I'm a peaceable man," just before he is provoked into shooting a bad guy. Despite his good intentions, which are frequently verbalized, he kills. He doesn't want to kill, but he has to; it's unavoidable. The major difference between the cowboys of the Hickok generation and the characters played by John Wayne is that Wayne's cowboys seem to enjoy killing more.

All Western heroes are caught in a similar dilemma. They don't want to kill, but they are well equipped if the necessity arises, and they are good at it. Bad guys bring disorder; good guys restore order by killing the bad guys. Good triumphs over evil.

Is this not, in miniature, a replica of our international relations? No one wants war, but it pays to be prepared. Some confrontations are unavoidable, and survival may require killing in self-defense.

It is time we recognized that war is part of the design of our culture, functionally related to our culture pattern not as a suspension of normal social relations but as an integral, if irrational, part of the whole. This has nothing to do with blaming individuals who are considered responsible for starting wars or continuing warfare. War is the natural outcome of the operation of our social system, just one more way aggression finds expression. The fact that warfare is elaborately and intricately woven into our social fabric has prevented us from seeing the obvious. As Will and Ariel Durant expressed it in *The Lessons of History*, published in 1968, "In the last 3421 years of recorded history, only 268 have seen no war." [4] Ours is a war culture. And the danger is that the controlled aggression that has made us so productive places at our disposal the opportunity for almost total catastrophe and, as has already been demonstrated, the inclination to use it.

No wonder the young are anxious. Raised on "Combat" and war movies, seeing the Vietnam war on TV, hearing the weekly tallies of the body count as if they were "scores in some hideous game," how could they be otherwise? Nuclear incineration is not science fiction, but an all too possible prospect.

No wonder we are in the midst of a new romanticism. If science and technology are the embodiment of reason, away with it. For the young, today's emotions offer a better guide for living than yesterday's tradition. Try the occult, read the

---

[4] Will and Ariel Durant, *The Lessons of History*, p. 81.

stars, try Yoga and Zen, get out the cards, meditate, encounter your self, roll in the grass, humanize our education, try to put your head together and find out where you're at. The reaction against reason, against established cultural norms is a flight from a "sickness" more often felt than rationally diagnosed. And it is important to realize that the reaction is also a part of the illness, not part of the cure.

Complementary to the aggression that is channeled into competition, into crime and violence, into inglorious wars, into domestic discord is the other central theme of our culture, love. As even a popular song recognizes, "What the world needs now is love, sweet love." Hippies and flower children, lost explorers in experimental communes, dropouts from the rat race, the new nomads are all symptomatic of a sense of love lost that they will somehow recover and restore. Like rotary antennas, our children turn this way and that in search of a saving love.

No wonder many of them have rediscovered Christianity. Its message of love, mercy, forgiveness, and salvation has offered emotional solace to millions. The code of conduct enjoined upon its members would save the world—if followed. The problem has always been that it has not been followed. Because, sadly, it cannot be followed.

If Kardiner's thesis is valid, Christianity contains the secret of Western character structure.* And that secret should explain why, with every good intention, we continue to fail to do what we know we ought to do. From Kardiner's point of view, Christianity is a religious institution that represents a projection of the emotional state of children reared thousands of years ago in the lands surrounding the eastern Mediterranean. Passed down through the generations, both the religion and the child-rearing practices are probably relatively intact—cultural practices in both areas

* Kardiner's interpretation of Christianity, which differs considerably from this one, can be found in his *The Psychological Frontiers of Society*.

being highly resistant to change and the span of time in anthropological terms being quite brief. That the religion is still so meaningful to so many suggests its emotional significance is relatively undiminished. And we still practice, "Spare the rod and spoil the child."

What has Christianity to reveal about the nature of Western man? To begin with, it is generally accepted that the fact that he is a male god points to our patrilineal tradition. Then, that he created the world and all it holds is a familiar creation myth. That the first man and woman lived in a paradise from which they were ejected suggests the imperfect world we all know and the perfect one we long for. That Adam and Eve were ejected because they sinned, the fall of man from grace, suggests a disobedient rebellion against an Almighty Father, inherited in all of us as a tendency to sin, to defy the Father. A proud, defiant son offends the Father who, to show his love for mankind, allows his only son Christ to be crucified in atonement for the sins of mankind. The Father loves his children despite their defiance and disobedience. Earlier, God had had a similar problem with his angels. A defiant angel who tried to lead a rebellion against Him was cast down into an underworld where as Satan he is responsible for most of the evil in the world.

Attempting to reconstruct the unrecorded emotional life of children long ago by working back from today's child-rearing practices and from our religious tradition is hazardous in the extreme. But I imagine a stern, demanding father who required, above all, obedience in his sons. Also, assuming a mixed agricultural-herding economy, the sons were being prepared to assume the burden of hard work in the fields and with the flocks. The discipline required of laborious work in the fields was reflected in the disciplining of his children with more falling on the sons than the daughters. Strong resentment of the father would reasonably follow. Add to this Freud's Oedipal drama where a repressive father overwhelms his helpless son. These are the conditions for an unconscious teeming with hatred and fear.

Assuming these to be the common emotions in the unconscious of those children, it follows that they might create a religious tradition where an all-powerful Father loves his errant children and forgives their sins. But that the Father as Son would allow himself to be crucified is a sacrifice signifying a surpassing love for his children. This extraordinary, unearthly compassion attributed to God conceals the depth of the hostility directed at earthly fathers. The denial of these feelings is accomplished by the mechanism of reaction formation whereby hatred for the father becomes transformed into a great love for fathers. It is this love which the Father of all returns, so pure a love that evil arises only from a fallen angel, a necessary spiritual adjunct for the God who is love. The need, the wish, the longing is for a loving father.

This is the secret of Christianity: a god of love whose worshipers are filled with unrecognizable hate and for that reason unable to live up to their Christian ideals and attributing lapses to sins prompted by devils, their own unconscious impulses. In this sense Christ did die for our sins, our *unconscious* sins. The result in our culture is that love is a special way of hating.

Only child-rearing practices that foster an uncommon number of aggressive impulses can explain the behavior of men and women in Western culture, then and now.* No one deliberately intends such a result, neither parent nor child. It just "happens." But how does it happen? Whiting and Child clarify the process. Look at their analysis of our child-rearing practices in relation to their data from other cultures. It's all there. The surging waves of hostility arise from our pattern of infant gratifications and frustration.

* In *The Psychological Frontiers of Society*, Kardiner expresses, erroneously I feel, the view that our child-rearing practices are mildly indulgent.

For a comparison group, Whiting and Child use data on child rearing gathered from a sample of fifty middle-class families who were living in Chicago in the 1940s.[5] The same judges who evaluated data from seventy-five other cultures rated our practices assigning numerical values for degree of indulgence and severity. When the judgments for oral indulgence in the Chicago sample were compared to judgments for fifty-one societies where data was available, the only culture that scored lower than the Chicago sample was the Marquesan! Doesn't this suggest that our anxiety over thumb-sucking is really anxiety over oral gratification, that a child who is allowed to indulge his impulses is endangered?

When comparisons were made of the age when weaning occurs, data from fifty-two cultures revealed that the only culture that scored lower than ours was again the Marquesan![6] Severity of weaning was not as markedly exceptional. The Chicago sample was judged to be in the middle of the upper half of thirty-nine cultures for degree of severity. The severity of our weaning practices is above average but not as striking as our proximity to Marquesan practices regarding oral frustration and early weaning.

The overall effect of denial of the breast has resulted not only in an initial frustration for the infant at a crucial early stage but, in addition, a rather exaggerated emphasis upon the female breast among American adults. I call it the triple H, the Hugh Hefner Hypothesis. The spectacular success of *Playboy* is based on marketing mammary glands to the masses, providing fantasy materials for older boys focused on the breasts boys were denied the opportunity to play with.

For anal indulgence, the Chicago sample again departs from the cross-cultural comparison of twenty-two societies. The only societies that are less indulgent than our own are the Chagga and the Tanala.[7] Comparisons of the age when

[5] John W. M. Whiting and Irvin L. Child, *Child Training and Personality: A Cross-Cultural Study*, p. 66.

[6] Ibid., p. 71.

[7] Whiting and Child, *Child Training*, p. 74.

toilet training begins places us lower than any other except for the Tanala. And for degree of severity in toilet training, the Chicago sample was given the same rating as the Tanala where obedience and wealth play as large a part as they do among ourselves.[8]

When comparisons were made for severity of socialization practices in the area of sexual behavior, separate judgments were assigned to masturbation and immodesty. Ratings of seventeen societies for initial indulgence of childhood masturbation range from a high of nineteen, which was received by the Alorese, to a low of eleven, received by the Manus. The American sample was rated at ten, the lowest of them all.[9] When socialization anxiety surrounding masturbation is the focal point for comparisons, the American sample scored the same as the most severe of the preliterate societies, the Manus.[10] Ratings for indulgence of immodesty found the American sample one point above the lowest preliterate society; whereas for severity of modesty training, the American sample was only one point below the median for preliterate societies.

We apply to the mutual hostility of our children the euphemism sibling rivalry. If you have ever witnessed the no-holds-barred ferocity of enraged brothers, you begin to suspect it is more than that. When Cain slew his brother Abel as reported in the Old Testament, Kardinerian echoes reverberate from then to now. The cruelty of our children toward each other is proverbial. Small children must be taught not to bite one another. The aggressive impulses that our child-rearing practices arouse have to be suppressed.

One of the characteristics of parent-child relations that Arnold Gesell documented in years of observations of American children are the periodic waves of rebelliousness that occur throughout childhood and that are especially

8 Ibid., p. 77.
9 Ibid., p. 79.
10 Ibid., p. 80.

evident among adolescents.[11,12] Why do these periodic up-heavals occur? Psychologists tend to attribute these episodes to independence training. Most children practice self-assertion until the time they are old enough to take their place in our society as self-reliant individuals.

Actually independence training is another euphemism for training in the management of aggressive impulses. Nothing equals the appeal of a human infant to its parents. The wonder is that all children do not become hopelessly dependent and remain with their parents always. Our culturally prescribed child-rearing patterns prevent such abnormal dependency most of the time. The norm is for individuals to set up their own household, the neolocal residential pattern. To enable children to be able to leave home and equally important, to enable parents to let them do so, we raise them from infancy with sufficient harshness to achieve the end result. It is our way and most of us consider our way the best way. It is part of the design of our culture. The children grow up and leave home. The parents try to build a new life without them. Visiting is obligatory and tinged with ambivalence, probably on both sides.

The greatest single influence upon our patterns of child rearing in the past two and a half decades has been Dr. Benjamin Spock. His book, *Baby and Child Care*, is second in sales only to the Bible. Yesterday's adolescents, often referred to as the Spock generation, presented us with a curious historical spectacle: no sight quite matched Dr. Spock marching at the head of a group of young people protesting the war in Vietnam. It is as if Spock were saying, "Stop killing my children!" And meaning just that. After all, he did spend his life in their service.

His book appeared in 1946, just in time for the postwar baby boom. And for so many new parents living some

[11] Arnold Gesell and Frances Ilg, *Child Development*, pp. 287–97.

[12] Arnold Gesell, Frances Ilg, and Louise Bates Ames, *Youth, the Years from Ten to Sixteen*, pp. 380–95.

distance from their own parents, Spock's guide proved to be the perfect pacifier. He was most reassuring when he urged parents to relax, examine the problem calmly, and if they needed assistance to call their local pediatrician.

The first Spock babies were becoming eighteen in 1964. In the years that followed, many thousands more joined them. They were the product of parents who were more indulgent, more permissive than earlier generations of parents. Not much more really when compared to patterns of child-rearing in more indulgent cultures, but more indulgent nevertheless.

What changes can be attributed to Spock's influence? I think the one that matters is that these middle-class youngsters have been called the love generation. They were less uptight than their elders. They were more open in their approach to each other: the boundary between self and other had a softer edge. And above all, they were tolerant of each other, willing to allow each to do his own thing whatever that might be.

The Spock influence was not so great that aggressive impulses were eliminated, but they were probably somewhat fewer than has been characteristic of American character. The rigid compulsion to conform still herded them in similar directions and rebelliousness now took on ideological overtones as the new romanticism urged many to return to a simple life of sharing. Tragically, their openness to new experience exposed many of them to devastating attempts to achieve salvation through chemistry, but Spock cannot be considered responsible for the new romanticism.

The peculiar development in Spock's influence is that he changed direction. He revised his book in 1957 to reject the charge of permissiveness. He later wrote that he had never intended to create conditions where a child victimizes its parents by unreasonable demands.[13] He was opposed to

---

[13] Benjamin Spock, "How My Ideas Have Changed," *Redbook*, p. 124.

spoiling a child through thoughtless indulgence.

If Spock's followers are still guided by his book, adolescents who reach eighteen in 1974 and thereafter should be more true to the American type. Certainly many parents escaped his influence altogether, although their children have been indirectly influenced by the example of their peers.

Still, the astonishing conclusion one is tempted to draw from Spock's reversal is that he was unaware of the effect of his work. Actually, if the number of aggressive impulses is ever going to be reduced in our culture, our children will have to be reared with more indulgence. He was on the right track but appears not to have known it.

Our culture will change. No doubt slowly and in its own sprawling way. But if it is to change in the direction of fewer aggressive impulses and all that that implies in terms of reduced interpersonal conflict and intergroup conflict, Spock has inadvertently pointed the way. Combined with the data ethnologists have brought back from remote corners of the world in their study of other cultures, there are possibilities.

We should rear our children with a love that engenders love, not with the severity that begets aggression. Every attempt should be made to gratify the infant's oral needs. The sensuous pleasures of breast-feeding should not be denied both mother and infant. When 90 percent of mothers are able to breast-feed and only 20 percent do, we are off to a bad start. Breast-feeding should provide the first opportunity for a bond of mutual affection to develop between the mother and her infant. At the same time, breast-feeding helps mothers. Mothers generally have one chance in twenty-five of developing breast cancer, but if she breast-feeds her infant for six months, her chances drop to one in one hundred twenty-five. Further, nursing helps her uterus contract after childbirth, preventing hemorrhaging. Nursing also helps her figure get back in shape and sometimes improves it.

How long should a mother nurse? I wonder. The impression I have from other cultures is at least a year and probably two. Many mothers in many other cultures nurse until a new infant is born, the last child being nursed longest. Weaning should be as gradual as circumstances allow.

Will such a child be spoiled? Apparently not. What really "spoils" the child is the denial of the warmth and intimacy that accompanies suckling.

Has the busy mother in a nuclear family the time to devote so much attention to her newborn? She doesn't have to work in the fields tending the crops. Presumably Western mothers have more leisure than any mothers have ever had. What better use for her leisure? After all, what are breasts for? Time must be found or made, if the cycle of deprivation is to be broken. Women who believe that they have more important work to do are mistaken, tragically mistaken. "The hand that rocks the cradle rules the world" turns out to be true after all. The quality of maternal care is the crucial variable. What the world needs least is less. Only women can disarm future generations.

Nor should the training of the child's sphincter controls be the occasion for punishing the child. The punished child longs for retaliation. Punish the child and every blow will haunt your future. Less anxious parents will make for less anxious children. Less angry parents will make for less angry children. Too early a start only multiplies frustration. Around two years old seems the best time to begin.

How can we apply this same attitude toward the child's sexual impulses? It goes against our grain. We probably cannot. It requires too fundamental a change. Nor does it appear to be necessary.

Our culture inhibits sexuality. Every culture defines appropriate sexual behavior for every age group, designating eligible partners from the ineligible. The totally free exercise of heterosexual impulses is only a fantasy. A relatively uninhibited culture was the Marquesan. Despite comparative freedom in heterosexual play during childhood and adolescence, aggression ran rampant in Marquesan culture. It was caused primarily by oral deprivation. Our aggression probably originates the same way. Frustration of sexual impulses, occurring later, would not by itself be a sufficient cause for marked aggression.

Loving parents will inhibit a child's sexual impulses in subtle ways without emotional scenes, recognizing their natural origin. More important than inhibited sexuality is the feeling parents have for their child. A loved child returns that same love; a rejected child, a hated child returns that same hate. The child who is loved one minute and hated the next is hopelessly confused in his emotions. That urge to punish "for his own good" must be guarded against. The child cannot know the difference. Punishment, in any form, only reveals the ambivalence of the parents and is prompted by their own unmanageable impulses or is institutionalized to preserve the past.

Our culture is drifting toward more freedom for sensual impulses under the influence of Freudian psychoanalysis. The delusion is that inhibited sexuality distorts personality and wreaks social havoc. Freud was the genius who first sorted out the affective systems in the developing child and theorized about the aftereffects of frustration. He found repressed libidinal impulses underlying many neurotic symptoms. But he also thought repressed sexuality the price of civilization. He favored social controls on sexuality for that reason. Repressed sexuality creates social order, not havoc. Havoc is wrought by uncontrollable aggression. The real face of evil is hatred, not repressed sexuality.

What may have happened is that in our original anxiety to inhibit sexual impulses, we generalized our efforts and attempted to inhibit any childhood impulses toward sensual gratification. As a culture, we overreacted.

The drift toward sexual freedom will not solve our problem. It may reduce the incidence of neurosis. It may also prove disruptive of established social norms. Insofar as warfare is an established social norm, we want to disrupt it. I don't think it necessary or desirable to disrupt the nuclear family.

The nuclear family has become a popular target for attack as if our ills are attributable to its fragile structure. Certainly the family is under many stresses, among them poverty, unemployment, and impersonal corporate transfers. Many wives resent their maternal roles and envy the career opportunities and experiences of their husbands. But the major strain on family life is that brought about by the personalities of family members. The aggression that our child-rearing fosters is denied expression outside the home. So it is inside the home that anger spills over between husband and wife and between parents and their children. Domestic strife seems magnified when there are no relatives nearby to turn to. Where anger is continually turned inward and constrained within the family, why should it be surprising that so many families finally explode.

The solution to our problem and to the major problem within the nuclear family is to rear children not filled with hatred. But how can one interrupt and alter a cultural process that resists change? Won't such a change take a long time? Is there enough time remaining? Won't we be overwhelmed by our enemies?

If enough people in the world understand the necessity for change, they will try. Our hopes have always rested with the next generation. Yes, it will take a long time, perhaps many generations. What else is there to do but try? The problem is now almost worldwide, wherever Western culture or its influence is dominant. If we move toward the solution together, we will find the world filled, not with enemies, only people.

One consequence of reduced aggressive impulses may be the most threatening of all. If our high level of material prosperity floats on a pool of sublimated aggression, the possibility exists that by changing our child rearing, we may pull the plug, and our wealth will go down the drain. That prospect is remote since we will still possess our accumulated heritage of skills and knowledge. And if the pace of innovation slackens, many think our natural resources will last longer.

On the other hand, if Freud is correct and sublimated sexuality drives our social engines, since no fundamental change in sexuality is suggested, there is nothing to fear. If that fails, there is still McClelland's need-achievement: task-oriented producers may solve our production problems. And finally, if all else fails, there will still be an open-class system to spur us onward and upward.

One prospect beckons that overshadows all risks even of reduced rewards: a world without war, without hatred, without man's inhumanity to man or woman or child.

Selected Bibliography

For ease of usage, the bibliography lists some references in more readily available editions and the date of the original edition in parentheses.

Adamson, Joy. *Born Free, A Lioness of Two Worlds*. New York: Pantheon, 1960.

Alland, Alexander. *The Human Imperative*. New York: Columbia University Press, 1972.

Ardrey, Robert. *African Genesis*. New York: Dell, 1967 (1961).

Ardrey, Robert. *The Territorial Imperative*. New York: Atheneum, 1966.

Barnouw, Victor. *Culture and Personality*. Homewood, Ill.: Dorsey Press, 1963.

Benedict, Ruth. *Patterns of Culture*. Boston: Houghton Mifflin, Sentry edition, n.d. (1934).

Berkowitz, Leonard. *Aggression: A Social Psychological Analysis*. New York: McGraw-Hill, 1962.

Bernard, L. L. *Instinct*. New York: Henry Holt, 1924.

Bohannon, Paul. *Africa and Africans*. Garden City, N.Y.: Natural History Press, 1964.

Buettner-Janusch, John. *Origins of Man*. New York: John Wiley, 1966.

Carmichael, Leonard. "The Development of Behavior in Vertebrates Experimentally Removed from the Influence of External Stimulation." *Psychological Review* 33 (1926): 51–58.

Coleman, James. *Abnormal Psychology and Modern Life*. 3rd ed. Glenview, Ill.: Scott, Foresman, 1964.

Crafts, L. W., et al. *Recent Experiments in Psychology*. New York: McGraw-Hill, 1960 (1938).

Darwin, Charles. *The Origin of Species*. New York: Literary Classics, Modern Library Edition, n.d., (1859).

Dennis, Wayne. *The Hopi Child*. New York: Appleton-Century, 1940.

Dollard, John, et al. *Frustration and Aggression*. New Haven: Yale University Press, 1968 (1939).

DuBois, Cora. *The People of Alor*. Minneapolis: University of Minnesota Press, 1944.

Durant, Will and Ariel. *The Lessons of History*. New York: Simon and Schuster, 1968.

Fletcher, Ronald. *Instinct in Man*. New York: International Universities Press, 1957.

Forde, C. Daryll. *Habitat, Economy and Society*. New York: Dutton, 1963 (1934).

Fortune, Reo. *Sorcerers of Dobu*. New York: Dutton, 1963 (1932).

Freud, Sigmund. *An Outline of Psychoanalysis*. New York: W. W. Norton, 1949.

Freud, Sigmund. *A General Introduction to Psychoanalysis*. Garden City, N.Y.: Doubleday, 1953 (1920).

Gesell, Arnold and Ilg, Frances. *Child Development*. New York: Harper and Row, 1949.

Gesell, Arnold; Ilg, Frances; and Ames, Louise Bates. *Youth, The Years from Ten to Sixteen*. New York: Harper and Brothers, 1956.

Golding, William. *Lord of the Flies*. New York: Harcourt, Brace, 1954.

Gorer, Geoffrey. *Himalayan Village*. New York: Basic Books, 1967 (1938).

Handy, E. C. *The Native Culture of the Marquesas*. Honolulu: Bishop Museum, no. 9, 1923.

Harlow, Harry and Harlow, Margaret. "Social Deprivation in Monkeys." *Scientific American* (November 1962), pp. 133–46.

Harris, Marvin. *The Rise of Anthropological Theory*. New York: Thomas Y. Crowell, 1968.

Herskovitz, Melville J. *Dahomey, An Ancient West African Kingdom*. New York: J. J. Hoguston, 1938.

Holmberg, Allan. *Nomads of the Long Bow*. Garden City, N.Y.: Natural History Press, 1969 (1950).

James, William. *Psychology*. New York: Fawcett, 1963 (1890).

Josephy, Alvin M. *The Indian Heritage of America*. New York: Bantam, 1969.

Kardiner, Abram. *The Individual and His Society*. New York: Columbia University Press, 1939.

Kardiner, Abram, et al. *The Psychological Frontiers of Society*. New York: Columbia University Press, 1945.

Kardiner, Abram and Preble, Edward. *They Studied Man*. New York: New American Library, Mentor edition, 1963.

Linton, Ralph. *The Cultural Background of Personality*. New York: Appleton-Century-Crofts, 1945.

Lorenz, Konrad. *On Aggression*. New York: Harcourt, Brace, World, 1966.

Macgowan, Kenneth and Hester, Joseph. *Early Man in the New World*. Garden City, N.Y.: Doubleday Anchor, 1962 (1950).

Mandelbaum, D., et al. *The Teaching of Anthropology*. Washington: American Anthropological Association, 1963.

Manis, Jerome and Clark, Samuel, eds. *Man and Society*. New York: Macmillan, 1960.

McClelland, David., et al. *The Achievement Motive*. New York: Appleton-Century-Crofts, 1953.

McClelland, David. *The Achieving Society*. Princeton, N.J.: Van Nostrand, 1961.

McClelland, David and Winter, David. *Motivating Economic Achievement*. New York: Free Press, 1969.

McDougall, William. *An Introduction to Social Psychology*. New York: Barnes and Noble, 1960 (1908).

Mead, Margaret. *Growing Up in New Guinea*. New York: William Morrow, 1966 (1930).

Mead, Margaret. *New Lives for Old*. New York: Dell, 1968 (1956).

Mead, Margaret. "Warfare: An Invention—Not a Biological Necessity." *Anthropology, A Human Science*. Selected Papers of Margaret Mead. New York: D. Van Nostrand, 1964.

Montagu, Ashley, ed. *Man and Aggression*. New York: Oxford University Press, second edition, 1974.

Morris, Desmond. *The Naked Ape*. New York: McGraw-Hill, 1967.

Oliver, Douglas L. *The Pacific Islands*. Garden City, N.Y.: Doubleday Anchor, 1961 (1951).

Peter, Prince of Greece and Denmark. *A Study of Polyandry*. The Hague: Mouton, 1963.

Raum, O. J. *Chagga Childhood*. London: Oxford University Press, 1940.

Scott, J. P. *Aggression*. Chicago: University of Chicago Press, 1958.

Schaffer, George. *The Mountain Gorilla*. Chicago: University of Chicago Press, 1963.

Simmons, L. W. *Sun Chief: The Autobiography of a Hopi Indian*. New Haven: Yale University Press, 1942.

Spock, Benjamin. *Baby and Child Care*. New York: Pocket Books, 1957 (1946).

Spock, Benjamin. "How My Ideas Have Changed." *Redbook*, Oct., 1963.

Storr, Anthony. *Human Aggression*. New York: Atheneum, 1968.

Suggs, Robert. *The Hidden Worlds of Polynesia*. New York: New American Library, Mentor edition, 1965 (1962).

Suggs, Robert. *Marquesan Sexual Behavior*. New York: Harcourt, Brace, 1966.

Textor, Robert. *A Cross-Cultural Summary*. New Haven, Conn.: Human Relations Area Files Press, 1967.

Thompson, Laura and Joseph, Alice. *The Hopi Way*. Chicago: University of Chicago Press, 1944.

Thorpe, W. H. *Learning and Instinct in Animals*. Cambridge, Mass.: Harvard University Press, 1963.

Tiger, Lionel and Fox, Robin. *The Imperial Animal*. New York: Holt, Rinehart & Winston, 1971.

Tylor, Edward B. *Primitive Culture*. London: John Murray, 1871.

Waters, Frank. *Book of the Hopi*. New York: Ballantine, 1969 (1963).

Whiting, John W. M. and Child, Irvin L. *Child Training and Personality: A Cross-Cultural Study*. New Haven: Yale University Press, 1962 (1953).

Index